Acknowledgments

Thank You:

To my family in Ohio, and Yuji and Nick in Los Angeles. To my associates at ASCAP, BMI, and SESAC for inviting me to interview their songwriters and composers; to Arthur Bernstein, Mark Featherstone-Witty, Ian Gardner, and Martin Isherwood at the Liverpool Institute for Performing Arts (LIPA); and to my students who inspired this text.

To my friends and colleagues: Luis and Gloria Villegas, Keo Woolford, Jeffrey Tennyson, Bobbi Marcus, Dan DeSouza, John and JoAnn Braheny, Scott and Denise Davis, Marta Woodhull, John Philip Shenale, David Edward Byrd, Joe Beserra, Richard Moll, Susan Wong, Armando Soria, Kenny Kerner, Guy Marshall, Brett Perkins, Denise Bradley, Martin Cervantes, Simon Barber, and David Quan. And to the amazing Karan Longbrake, whose energy has inspired me since high school.

Thanks to Mike Lawson at ArtistPro and to my diligent editor, Dan Foster. Appreciation always to Mark Garvey, who first convinced me that I was an author.

Grateful thanks to Tena Clark and the staff at Disc Marketing/DMI Networks and Firehouse Recording Studios in Pasadena, California, with special gratitude to Ronny Schiff, whose support is immeasurable.

Selected interviews in this book were conducted for "Song Biz Profiles" and feature stories written for *Music Connection* magazine. Thank you to senior editor Mark Nardone, publishers Eric Bettelli and J. Michael Dolan, and associate editor Michael Mollura. The profile of Lindy Robbins appeared in *Songwriters Market 2005*. Thank you to editor Ian Bessler and Writer's Digest Books.

About the Author

Dan Kimpel is one of the American media's foremost authorities on popular music and songwriters. He contributes to a dizzying variety of print and electronic mediums, including books, interactive CDs, magazines, Web sites, videos, and new media. If you fly United Airlines worldwide, you can hear his audio interviews with hit recording artists and songwriters on The United Entertainment Network. Dan conducts workshops on the subject of music business networking at universities, conferences, and seminars across North America and in England. Visit Dan's Web site at www.dankimpel.com

Contents

Introduction XI

CHAPTER 1   **Personal Paths in the Music Business**. 1
The Kind of Person.... 2
Assessing Your Strengths. 3
Songwriters 3
Musicians 4
Music Biz Pro's: Aspiring Moguls 5
Technical Triumphs. 6
Born to Succeed. 7
Reinvention 9
Signs from the Universe. 10
The Commitment Key. 12
Time Has Come Today 13
Summary. 15

CHAPTER 2   **The Modern Music Business** 16
Transmission Is Secondary 16
Expanding and Contracting Genres 17
The New Music Entrepreneurs 18
Music for Kids 19
Soundtrack to a Fast Track 20
Internet Notions 22
Fish or Fowl? 23
A Mosaic of Mediums 25
Radio Is Our Salvation. 27
Satellite, Public, and Internet Radio. 31
chris and thomas: Acoustic Essence. 33
Music Publishing: The Way In. 35
Major and Indie Labels 37

Music Biz Marionettes: Who Pulls the Strings? 38
Validation 39
American Idolization. 40
Summary. 42

CHAPTER 3   **Personalities Plus** 43
Ten Successful Attributes of Music Biz Professionals 43
Negative Notions. 49
The Put Down 51
Negative to Positive 52
Find Reasons to Feel Good about Yourself. 54
Visualize Your Success. 54
Network with People You Respect and Observe
     Their Traits 55
The Smooth Road 55
Myths 57
Reinvention 58
Same Old Same Old. 59
Summary. 60

CHAPTER 4   **True Tales** 62
The I's Don't Have It 62
The Power of "You" 63
Could'a, Should'a, Would'a 64
You're It. 66
Bridges Aflame 67
Celebrity 68
Ten Strategies for Interacting with Celebrities 69
How Would I Reach You? 71
Who Needs You? 72
Look Around. 74
Sixth Sense 75
Drugs in the Music Biz 76
On the Road with John Mayer 77
Am I Too Old to Rock? 78

Critical Crises and Drama Queens 81
Ten Networking Strategies for Dispelling a Crisis 83
Treat Everyone with Respect 84
Summary. 86

CHAPTER 5   **Making Contact** 87
Body Language 87
Good Grooming 89
Clothes Horse 90
Ups and Downs in the Capitol Tower 91
Ten Visual Cues for Your "Look". 93
Conversation Instigation 94
Ten Conversation Leaders 95
Sensitive Areas. 97
Assumptions to Avoid about Anyone to Whom You're
        Introduced 98
Complimentary Consideration 98
Remembering Names 100
Did You Drop That Name? 101
Business Cards. 102
Working the Room 103
Hidden Opportunities. 106
Practice Makes Perfect. 108
The Fine Art of the Studio Hang 109

CHAPTER 6   **Telephone and E-Mail**. 112
The Telephone. 113
Sound 114
Reflections of Power 115
Telephone Basics 116
Telephone Tracking. 117
Cell Phones: Antennas of Satan? 118
Cell Phone Etiquette 121
E-Mail. 122

CHAPTER 7 **Creating Effective Tools of the Trade** 125

Press Kits. 126

The Folder 127

The Cover Letter 127

A CD or DVD 128

The Bio 129

Your Photo 133

Full-Court Press 134

Credibility in the Credits. 136

The Man in the Gorilla Suit. 138

Extreme Strategies. 139

Rejection 140

Ten Thoughts on Overcoming Rejection 141

Ten Reasons Your Calls Are Not Returned 142

Web-Wise 145

Do I Need a Web Site?. 146

Additional Resources. 151

CHAPTER 8 **Live Venues and Ventures**. 153

Gigology 101. 153

Creative Outlets. 154

Alternative Venues. 156

Inventing Your Own Show. 157

Soft Ticket. 157

How to Make a Soft Ticket Show Work for You 158

You Sounded Fabulous!. 159

Ten Post-Performance Tips 159

Performance Peeves. 160

Ten Commandments of Club Land 161

Club Clues. 162

Soundman Scenarios. 163

Scams 164

Compilation CDs. 166

Performing Rights 169

CHAPTER 9	**Success Stories**	172
	Jeffrey Steele: Country Craftsman	173
	Lindy Robbins: Late Bloomer	178
	Luis Resto: Lost in the Music	183
	Bob Malone: Road Warrior	185
	Summary	187
CHAPTER 10	**Go Where You Wanna Go**	188
	Nashville	189
	New York	193
	Los Angeles	196
	Emerging Cities	200
	All Over the Map	201
	Music Conferences	201
	15 Tips to Maximize Your Conference Experience	202
	World Beat	204
	Further Afield	205
CHAPTER 11	**Defining Your Direction**	207
	Questions for Artists	208
	Questions for Aspiring Moguls	210
	Teamwork	212
	Management	212
	When Do You Need a Manager?	213
	What to Look for in a Manager	214
	Do You Want to Be a Manager?	215
	Your Lawyer	215
	Agents	216
	Your Publicist	217
	Artist's Responsibilities	218
	Get a Job	219
CHAPTER 12	**It's a Wrap**	221
	Creative Confluence	221
	Five Tips for Personal References	222

Back Home 223
Making It Happen Where You Are 224
What Have You Been Given? 226
In Conclusion 227

Appendix A

Resources 229

Introduction

Who you know, what you know, and who knows you: Every single deal I've ever seen go down in the music business has been the direct result of a personal contact. In this way, the music business is not that different from any other enterprise because people will do business with those whom they know, whom they trust, and who they believe will deliver what is required and expected of them under any circumstance. In many other ways, however, the music business is radically different from other industries. It's built on a vibe; it's tied to trends, fashion, and media; it communicates an intangible commodity capable of mirroring profound emotions.

What Is a Networking Strategy?

Networking is communication—simple human interaction. *Strategy* is the art of devising or employing plans toward a goal. It follows that *Networking Strategies* are plans toward a successful career via personal relationships. Truth be told, it's always a new music business—the most significant recent changes have been the merger of the major record companies, the rise of independent labels and artists, and the leveling of the playing field through the Internet. Although all of these changes are significant, success will still be determined by personal relationships. I repeat: Every single deal I've ever seen go down in the music business has been a direct result of a personal contact.

This book is intended as a guide to making your personal strengths and relationships with others work for you. It's about connecting to others who share your aspirations, energies, and enthusiasm, and allowing these collective talents to shine for all, whether you're a professional or an aspirant in the music business: a songwriter, recording artist, musician, composer, music editor, music educator, music publisher, DJ, publicist, PR expert, entertainment lawyer, or if you plan on working with any of the above.

Raging Rivers and Tiny Ants

An upbeat, positive attitude, a sense that all will work out well in the world, and a drive to evolve, progress, and succeed in the music business are all attitudes that will light your path. Our destinies are self-fulfilling prophecies and the positive energy we transmit via our music will return amplified and multiplied.

That said, our ability to control the course of our specific destiny may be questionable. I was in Nashville interviewing songwriter and vocalist extraordinaire Michael McDonald when he offered this analogy: "Imagine a raging river; down through the rapids comes a 100-foot-long log moving at incredible speed. At the front of the log is perched a tiny ant who looks out and marvels, 'Man, I'm really driving this thing!'"

Who Am I?

I'm a music business survivor who has survived and flourished through a career that has taken me from the hard scrabble bars of Ohio to the power centers of Nashville, London, Tokyo, New York, and Hollywood.

For the past two and a half decades I've made my home in Los Angeles where my career trajectory includes phases as a songwriter and musician, a manager and publicist, creative director, event producer, journalist, editor, lecturer, and author. I continue to invent new outlets that reflect my love of music and songwriters and to utilize and expand my knowledge in an ever-shifting field.

I'm a strong believer that like the tiny ant in the story, we cannot *make* things happen; we can only put ourselves in a position *where* things will happen. Case in point: When I penned my first book, *Networking in the Music Business*, I was not an author; indeed, at that point I had barely published any articles. What I had was a pivotal position with a non-profit organization, a growing list of stellar contacts, and boundless enthusiasm for the subject.

Under the ministrations of a patient editor, I learned how to write a book. I was subsequently invited to travel across the U.S. and Canada to lecture at music conferences and institutions, but I soon figured out that someone who was an expert on personal contacts in the music business would be best served by using these talents to advance his own career, rather than making a questionable living foisting his views, and his words, on impressionable readers.

As creative director for the National Academy of Songwriters, I was honored to work with many of the greatest singer/songwriters in the history of American popular music: Joni Mitchell, John Fogerty, Tom Petty, Robbie Robertson, Gamble and Huff, Ashford and Simpson, Jackson Browne, and Burt Bacharach. I wrote, edited, produced, created, and made invaluable contacts.

Alas, the destiny of non-profit organizations is a treacherous one, and after three years I departed my cushy corner office on the 10th floor of a Sunset Boulevard high-rise, and moved my operations to my home in the hills of the Los Angeles district known as Eagle Rock.

Remember what I said about being in a position where things could happen? A continent away, at the Liverpool Institute for Performing Arts (LIPA), the college founded by Sir Paul McCartney, the head of music, Arthur Bernstein, dropped into the school library to find a book to read on a train trip. He grabbed mine. The next day he sent me a fax, inviting me to come to England to teach a one-week master class based on my book to LIPA's graduating seniors. This turned into a five-year venture, and expanded my realm of international contacts, if not my appreciation for British food, immeasurably.

Who Are You?

Sadly, the people who need this book the most will never read it. You know them: they're the ones who are too hip for the room; who bluster their way about, often using their aggression or belligerence to mask fears and uncertainties, always remaining clueless. I remember a call from a singer/songwriter in Arizona when the *Networking* book was first released. "All this networking is OK for some people, but I just want to stay in my studio, write songs, record, and get paid." Me too! But the caller never told me how to get that gig. I suspect he didn't know either.

The Power of Yes

I learned long ago in the music business, when someone asks you if you can do something, the correct answer is "Yes!" I'm not talking about jumping out of airplanes if you're afraid of heights or playing a classical toccata if you're a speed metal guitarist, but within the realm of reason, the possibilities others see in us often exceed the limitations we see in ourselves.

In order to do the gig, you have to get the gig; in order to get the gig, you have to understand the gig. If you aspire to a position at a record label, a publishing firm, or a performing rights organization, you will seldom see these positions advertised in the paper or anywhere online. Why? Because they will be filled by people from the inside of the business, never the outside.

My career took another dramatic leap when a longtime friend, Ms. Ronny Schiff, VP of audio programming for Disc Marketing (now DMI Entertainment Networks), asked me to conduct an audio interview with the classic British rockers, the Moody Blues, for a program to be heard worldwide by United Airlines passengers on The United Entertainment Network. Since then, I've conducted hundreds of interviews for United, speaking in studio to everyone from Leonard Cohen to Holland/Dozier/Holland to Brian Wilson and Rufus Wainwright. From legendary Rock Hall of Fame inductees to the hottest new band, it's my pleasure to interview them all. Had I not known Ronny socially, this incredible opportunity never would have arisen.

Over time, I've become the "go-to" guy for songwriter-related mediums. In print, *Music Connection* magazine, a bi-weekly West coast music publication, has been a welcome home for my prose, as I contribute the column, "Song Biz," and a profile of a songwriter, composer, or singer/songwriter to every issue as well as cover stories and feature interviews. I estimate I've interviewed over 200 hit makers for this magazine. I write and interview for all three U.S. Performing Rights organizations, ASCAP, BMI, and SESAC, and I've been conducting on-camera interviews for ASCAP's Pop, Film and Television, and Rhythm & Soul Awards, quizzing, on camera, everyone from Elvis Costello to Clint Eastwood.

I love to say yes. When ASCAP, BMI, or SESAC asks me to moderate a conference panel, I never ask, "How much does it pay?" Whether or not there's a check involved, I'm always glad to be of service. The visibility of these endeavors, the introductions to hit writers, and the credits are of far greater value to me than a few hundred dollars.

Dedicated to the Gig

Sometimes when people react to how busy I always seem, I have to remind them of this truth: When you don't have a job, you have to work extra hard.

I had to invent my career because it never existed; it is singular to me, but it's the people within my extensive world of contacts that have made it possible. I have always made it my creed to deliver above and beyond what was expected and to do it with joy. In the real world—that is, outside the entertainment sphere—we often encounter an attitude that is much less than 100 percent committed. At the store, the post office, the car wash, or wherever we interact with others, don't you sometimes have the feeling that those who work there are simply going through the motions—sleepwalking until quitting time?

The music business is not like this. It's made up of passionate, energetic, super-charged individuals who dedicate themselves totally to their craft and cause. Executives well into their fifth decades begin the day with a personal trainer or a five mile run before strapping on the headset for a round of calls to the East coast. Successful managers are combing the clubs on the Sunset Strip, checking out bands and artists until the wee hours, then making it to the Farmer's Market for a power breakfast. Recording engineers are taking advantage of free studio time to develop their own projects. Songwriters are collaborating for hours perfecting a line. Indie bands are scouring the hinterlands in vans, sleeping on fans' floors, and enlisting street teams to spread the news. They're not looking at their watches, waiting for quitting time, or waiting for the proverbial "something to happen."

In the changing course of our business, the only constant is our commitment to our career and the support of those around us. In the context of these pages it is my sincere intention to offer options, possibilities, affirmation, inspiration, and the occasional harsh slap of reality.

Be True to Yourself

I suspect that you, dear reader, already have many of the tools of communication to help you succeed. You're interested enough in honing your people skills—and understand how vital this is—that you've chosen to read this book. Please note: I never encourage anyone to be anyone other than who they are. *Networking Strategies* does not involve transforming yourself into another entity, becoming some manipulative, reptilian creature or disguising yourself in any way; rather, it's about taking the most positive aspects of yourself and projecting them to others.

I'd like to conclude this Introduction with a brief list of precepts that define my overall philosophy. Talent, information, and ability are all necessary ingredients for developing a career, but "people power" will ultimately determine your success.

Precepts of Networking Strategies

1. Be the person others want to help succeed.
2. Your objective is a long career; play a long-range game.
3. Treat everyone with equal respect.
4. Understand others, not only their words, but emotions.
5. Fame and fortune are not synonymous.
6. Your happiness in life is not dependent on either of the above.
7. Change is good.
8. At the crossroads of technology and show business is opportunity.
9. Play the game you truly believe you can win.
10. Project yourself with genuine, positive energy.

CHAPTER 1

Personal Paths in the Music Business

Every networking trick in the book will not help you if you do not have the goods. I don't claim to be able to improve your chops as a musician, your word flow as a songwriter, or your business acumen as a music biz whiz. However, if you have the necessary talents and continue to develop them, you will ultimately find a way to express yourself and build a viable career.

As I mentioned in my Introduction, my personal path in the music business began in my hometown and ultimately led me to all three music capitals and to Europe. As a boy, I dreamt of rocking stadiums, endless accolades, unfathomable riches. As a struggling musician dealing with shady club owners, elusive agents, and bare-bones tours in rusted out vans, I kept this image in my mind, but it grew fainter and was replaced by another image: a signpost inquiring "What talents have you been given and what are you doing with them?" It's a deep question. What do you think you were put on this earth to do?

The Kind of Person...

The most powerful character trait you can possess in the music business is being the kind of person others want to see succeed. There is no substitute for this quality and no way to manufacturer it synthetically because it's an inner strength.

To be effective, successful interaction in the music business must benefit both parties equally. This concept is based on the radio call letters "WIFM," which is broadcasting the question, "What's in it for me?" Fortunately, if you're just beginning your career, you probably have strengths that may not be immediately apparent to you: for instance, your level of enthusiasm and power of potential. As we progress in our careers, sometimes the joy of creating music, or being around those who do, becomes obscured or diluted. Meeting someone who is energized about what they're creating and who is on an upward career trajectory because of it, can be inspiring. This is one of the reasons I enjoy teaching and lecturing, because it gives me special opportunities to meet those who are coming up. And make no mistake: The music business thrives on new blood.

Not everyone in the music business is like this, however. I have longtime friends in the industry who seem to have disconnected from cultivating this quality, preferring instead to work only with those with whom they've worked over the years. In my opinion, this leads to stagnation. I feel that at any given moment there might be an airplane landing at LAX with someone getting off of the plane whom I should meet. And I probably will.

Assessing Your Strengths

So if you have enthusiasm, are the kind of person others want to see succeed, and believe that a life in music is your calling, how do you proceed? First, what do you love to do most? Second, what are your skill levels?

Knowledge-based skills are generally acquired from education and experience. These include computer skills, languages, and technical or musical abilities, to name a few. *Transferable skills* are portable skills that you take with you, such as communication and people skills, analytical problem solving, and planning. Equally important, *personal traits* are your own special qualities, which can include being dependable, flexible, friendly, hard working, expressive, formal, punctual, and a team player.

Songwriters

Are you capable of creating words and music that move a wide audience? Are you directing your energies into your songs and, at the same time, finding outlets for your music? Remember that what exists at the core of your songs—the intent and belief—are the qualities that resonate the strongest. By accepting special songs into the rarefied stratosphere of hits, however, buyers of music continually remind songwriters, "Don't write about *your* life—write about *mine*." Often, experiences that are the most personal are paradoxically the most universal as well.

Songwriting is all about collaboration. It's no secret—just look at the *Billboard* charts: co-written songs

3

rule the marketplace. How and why these collaborations exist—and what makes certain combinations work—are subjects of strong opinions, heated debate, mercenary judgments, and a certain amount of cosmic songwriter *juju* (mystical beliefs) . The trio of genres that currently comprises the majority of record sales—R&B (including hip-hop, which often has lists of collaborators because of the use of samples), country, and pop—are all overwhelmingly dominated by groups of writers. Choosing the right partner, or partners, is probably the most crucial decision a songwriter will make.

How do you meet collaborators? If you live in a music capital, you have the advantage of endless classes, workshops, panels, and seminars. If you live outside of New York, Nashville, and Los Angeles, you may have to work harder, but it's still possible to make contacts. I'll address the best ways to do so later in the book.

Networking Strategy for Songwriters

Songwriters are sometimes indistinguishable from the public at large. Songwriting organizations in your area are a great way to make local contacts. Online, check out www.justplainfolks.com.

Musicians

The music business is the most cooperative of endeavors. Sure, maybe you can play solo or perform exclusively at karaoke bars, but sooner or later you'll need to include other players to expand your sound.

Playing in a band can be a profoundly challenging experience and, of course, can be equally rewarding. Some bands in the history of pop music, such as The Rolling Stones and U2, are long-lived. Most often, however, a band will be a unit that you perform with for a short time until you leave or the band breaks up, and you continue on your way.

Networking Strategy for Hanging Out

Your local music store is a great place to interact. Ask the clerks for advice; they're probably players themselves and totally "plugged in." Post ads online or in local papers to make contacts. Sit at your favorite coffeehouse with a copy of a guitar, bass, or percussion magazine prominently arranged on the table and see who begins talking to you because of it. Wear T-shirts that display the logo of music manufacturers.

Music Biz Pros: Aspiring Moguls

The music business might be viewed as a pyramid, with large numbers of people and resources supporting the tiny fraction of artists who go on to be hugely successful. If you work in the business, you must adjust as it transforms itself and develop new skills to go with the flow. In many ways, if you're in a support position in this business, then you are possibly in the best position to ascend in the industry. I recall being in a class on artist management at UCLA Extension (a great place to meet people, by the way) observing a panel of eminent lawyers, agents, managers, and record execs, when one of them stated flatly, "The only people who have long careers in the music business are sitting up here."

Networking Strategy for the Energetic but Economically Challenged

Volunteer to help coordinate a music conference or event. You'll be in a position to make valuable contacts from the inside. However, never let your primary responsibility slide; you are not there simply to hype yourself, but to help the event. Still, it's a tried and true way of meeting others.

Technical Triumphs

Teaching in colleges, I encounter some students who are full-fledged musicians but who don't play conventional musical instruments. The tools of their trade are samplers, ProTools, and similar studio gadgetry. DJs and remixers are experiencing unprecedented prominence in the music business. In Europe, dance music rules, and in the urban centers of the U.S., the latest trends are often delivered by club savvy DJs.

The palette of creation has been widened dramatically by technology and sampling, and this has been a boon for many songwriters. It's not uncommon to see a writer who penned an R&B chestnut in the late '60s or early '70s being honored as a co-writer for Song of the Year by the performing rights organizations because a sample of the song was used in the latest Beyonce smash.

Networking Strategy for Studio Wizards

Studio and technical people are generally more at home behind the mixing board than in social situations. I recently lectured to a group of audio engineering students at a college in Sacramento who had requested that I help polish their networking skills for the Audio Engineering Society convention in San Francisco. Having worked with some of the most prolific engineers in Los Angles, I've observed that one common trait is a sense of quiet assurance, sympathy, and concentration. If engineering or studio work is in your future, you can't go wrong with studies of basic psychology. In addition, the most effective engineers I know are also proficient musicians.

Born to Succeed

I always ask the students to whom I lecture where they rank in birth order. This has become a new area of study and is an intriguing barometer of personality. In a collaborative situation—particularly in a band—birth order can make a huge difference in the interaction of the various personalities.

The oldest child often has the weight of expectations placed on him by his well-meaning parents. Oldest children are often moody and occasionally lack sensitivity. They can be intimidating, particularly by pushing people too hard or refusing to take no for an answer. Oldest children gravitate toward positions of responsibility: corporate heads, doctors, ministers, and band leaders. Almost all of the U.S. presidents were either the first-born child or the first-born son in their family, and all but two of the first astronauts sent into space were first-borns, and the other two were "only children." Often the eldest is also responsible for his or her siblings, so they learn to give orders. In the music biz, many producers and recording artists are oldest children.

Middle children are often mediators, adept at bridging opinions. Middle children have the ability to see both sides of the story, to empathize with a diversity of opinions, and often to peacefully resolve potentially disruptive conflicts. Middle children may feel they have the most negative lot in life and are less than special when, in essence, they have the best of both worlds. Middles tend to make friends easily. Once they have them, they often work harder to keep them. They're usually good at keeping secrets, too. Middle children may gravitate to positions as musicians, lawyers, or artist managers.

An exercise that usually impresses classes I teach is when I correctly predict that the majority of the students are the youngest children in their families. The reason is quite simple: Youngest children, to compete with their older siblings, often use clowning or other entertainment to call attention to themselves. The down side is that they may expect others to make their decisions or take responsibilities, but they are many times overachievers, using every means at their disposal to compete with their older siblings. Later-borns tend to be more creative and much more likely to reject the status quo. Many performers are youngest children.

Only children are often self centered, in their younger years not as effective in relationships with other children, but more at home with adults, so they can often be confident and well spoken. Only children are usually not afraid to make decisions and are comfortable with their opinions. They generally like things to be organized and are often on time. Often they can be the most creative of all.

The above scenarios are not meant as empirical scientific facts. Moreover, any character trait that is negative can certainly be recognized and muted as need be.

Reinvention

In biology (not my strong suite, I assure you) we learn that cells mutate and change in order to survive. A successful music business career should be emotionally fulfilling and hopefully a long one, but what we want as children—glory, riches, etc.—is generally supplanted at some point by a desire for stability, contentment, and a sense that we're doing something right in the world.

The music business is not, and has never been, a stable environment. Changes are sweeping and huge. Artists have become the most disposable part of the equation, yet paradoxically, it is the artists who drive the business and remain at its center. Around them swirls every imaginable participant, from the lawyer who signs them, to the makeup artist who makes them look good for the camera, to the roadie who changes their guitar strings.

The choices of careers in the music business are incredible. The outside public sees only the artist, but we as music business insiders know that there are legions of hard-working, creative souls who are propping them up and propelling them forward.

So what happens to artists after they exceed their 15 minutes of fame? They might produce records, write songs, develop talent, open recording studios, or become record label executives. Remember, they're already inside the business, so they can move laterally if they so choose.

Long-term practitioners in the music business will most likely have more than one career. Beginning as musicians, love and understanding of the music will create more options. Having spent many years in the trenches as a songwriter and musician, I know what its like to call my answering machine and sing a fragment of a song I don't want to forget, to have a song placed "on hold" interminably, to have a track with a major artist be taken off the record a week before its release. Most important, I know the miracle of a seamless verse and a melody that seems to have written itself. This experience is invaluable in interviewing songwriters.

I consider myself a songwriter, even though I no longer write songs. I prefer to express myself now through prose, which allows me many more words to say what I want to say. But when I write prose I still think as a songwriter: I concentrate on an intro, a second verse that moves the story foreward, and a bridge that takes the message upwards, and I always remember the songwriters mantra of "Don't bore us, Doris, get to the chorus."

Signs from the Universe

I had a recent conversation with a young man I'd met when he was an electronica composer/performer in Los Angeles, who informed me that he is now pursuing his new career as an actor. "The universe sent me signs," he told me. He was paraphrasing words he heard me deliver at a lecture, and flattered as I was that he could quote me, it inspired me to revisit the message behind this directive.

At one point in my life, worn down by performing in clubs, I decided to take a respite from playing live music. All well and good, but I still needed to pay the bills. I applied for a low-level part-time public relations gig and, as the saying goes, the veil was lifted—I realized that I had an untapped reservoir of talents and abilities. I subsequently returned to the music business on the other side of the desk with much greater reward. The universe had sent me a sign.

Years later, I was managing Keo Woolford, an artist from Hawaii. Despite the power of his charisma, songwriting, and conceptual abilities, we were having a rough time getting him signed to a record deal. However, we were approached by a prestigious Los Angeles theater who inquired if Keo would be willing to write and perform a one-man piece based on his Hawaiian origins for a segment of a multi-artist performance. Although he was skeptical ("But I'm a singer," I remember him saying), I convinced him that this was an unprecedented opportunity. The show was a smash. *The Los Angeles Times* theater critic raved, the show was held over, and suddenly the young man who thought he was a singer became a sought-after actor. A nice coda: I saw him perform to an audience of 1,500 starring in a revival of *The King and I* at the London Palladium. He now lives in New York and continues to break new ground as an actor and a writer. And, yes, he writes songs. He also contributed to a project nominated for a recent Grammy for Reggae Album of the Year.

Things that happen of significance in the entertainment world often happen naturally and easily. There is no science involved—it's a vibe; they just feel right. Your instincts will tell you—if you've been trying to knock down doors for years with your songs and your music, maybe it's time to step back, be quiet, and listen.

The Commitment Key

One situation that often comes up in the course of my lectures and consultations is that I meet artists or songwriters who define their career trajectories this way: "I was a professional musician. I was out of it for awhile. Now I'm getting back into it. Do you think I have a chance to make it?"

Let's define our terms. Does "make it" mean to obtain a record deal, to make a living as a musician or songwriter, or to find a way to share something special with an audience? If it's the third alternative, the answer is probably "Yes."

If someone is working a full-time job and supporting a family and has a fully developed career outside of music, she can probably write songs in her spare time and play weekend shows, but will her future be compromised by her present level of comfort?

Recording artists tend to be signed at progressively younger ages. Who else could live in a van, tour across the country eating frozen burritos at 7-11 stores, survive on three hours of sleep on a fan's floor, and dedicate their entire existence to living and breathing music? They're out there in America touching audiences. And as a rule they don't have wives or husbands and kids at home needing to be fed.

In my experience, people who are successful in the music biz don't have other options. They don't choose music; the music chooses them. While it's certainly not my place to tell people what they can and cannot do, I truly believe the music business will never be a canoe that we can blithely enter and exit at will. It moves down a roaring river. When we step out it travels on torrents, far beyond our reach.

And you can never get out of a business that you were never really in. At some point, you'll have to grab that paddle, face the rapids, and push off.

Networking Strategies is about having the fortitude and foresight to weather the changes, create a niche only you can fill, and establish a real audience for your music and a bullet-proof list of close personal contacts.

Those of us who stay in the business have often made tremendous sacrifices to do so. Maybe we've watched while members of our peer group have taken lofty corporate positions, purchased palatial homes, and made six-figure incomes. But keep in mind that we can never compare our lives to that of any other person. We're each singular—and we have only one life to live, our own. If the music chooses us, then it's up to us not only to find a way to survive, but to thrive.

Time Has Come Today

There is the concept of an artist, and the concept of an artist in his time. Timing is crucial to wide-scale artistic acceptance. Look at the famous historical model, the Beatles. The group was introduced in the U.S. at a critical time—President John F. Kennedy had been assassinated, and the country was undergoing severe depression and anxiety. What better to dispel the gloom than four sunny boys from Liverpool brimming with hope and melody?

The biggest artists often express values in direct opposition to the times in which they live. Elvis rose during the Eisenhower era. During the strait-laced, conservative Wall Street values of the Reagan administration, the omni-sexual antics of Madonna provided a welcome counterpoint. During the optimism of the Clinton administration, dark grunge flourished. Political hip-hop, of course, and the melding of metal and rap have flowered under the political climate of George W. Bush.

This is not to say that you should alter your musical/artistic approach to take advantage of the sociological edge, only that you should be well aware of it. I was recently on a panel at the University of Southern California (USC) with Marshall Altman, A&R, Columbia Records. "The more you chase the music business the further away it becomes," he shared.

What Marshall meant was this: If there is a current trend, and you reinvent yourself in an attempt to be a part of it, by the time you've written songs and recorded them and costumed/pierced/tattooed/dyed yourself to conform, another new trend will have supplanted what you're trying to emulate, and you'll look cheesy and outdated. Worse, you'll have no credibility, since what you were trying to portray in the first place wasn't even you.

The second you see a bandwagon, it's too late to jump on it. Pop music is cyclic—if you do what you believe in, eventually the cycle will come around to you.

Summary

If creativity doesn't have an outlet, a path, it stagnates at a dead-end. True creativity is not defined simply by the ability to create art, but in divining outlets for it. It's through our interactions with others as a part of a community that we begin to modify and monitor our own success. As our contacts move up, we also rise.

CHAPTER 2

The Modern Music Business

The modern music business reinvents itself with blinding speed, and those of us who stay abreast the changes and are adaptable to new technologies, new genres of music, and new artists can always invent new methods of using our talents. In this chapter you'll meet some key industry players who have not only weathered these changes but have turned them to their advantage.

Transmission Is Secondary

From wax to digital transmission, the music business has always been in drastic technological flux. At a lecture I attended in Liverpool, Sir George Martin related that when he began his career, weights were dropped from the ceiling and the resultant motion was what made wax mastering discs go around—machines were too unreliable. Sir George is now a principal owner of AIR Studios, a facility that boasts satellite technology enabling music recorded on their sound stage in London to be immediately sync'd to picture in Hollywood. It's a long way from the post-war ropes and pulleys of the past.

CDs, iPods, BlackBerries, ring-tones, and whatever comes next is not what this book is about. As drastic as the changes in technology may seem, what is vital to understand is the power of the people who make the music and run the music business. It's an arena in which the wildcard often comes into play, and something that is totally unexpected, and real, breaks through.

Expanding and Contracting Genres

If artists are willing to do the work, the corresponding good news is that it is possible to find an audience for almost any type of music. New genres are constantly being invented: from emo to children's music, Americana to electronica, and beyond. Niche markets make it possible for literally any genre to flourish, but like any other commodity-based business, you have to locate the audience of buyers for your music. In recent years, hip-hop has moved from underground street music to dominate the mainstream. Rock in all forms will always have a place, and its convergence with hip-hop via creative "mash-ups" and new styles that merge the intensity of metal to the urban verbal expression attract fans of both styles. Both rock and hip-hop are people's music.

Neither rock nor hip-hop is a conservative form; their shared roots are in outlaw cultures, but over time both have been appropriated by the mainstream. Both forms are decidedly global—you can even hear Japanese and Korean rappers emulating the gangstas of South Central Los Angeles.

Pop music will always have a place in our pantheon of styles. Currently the strongest market for pop is with "tweens"—that is, young listeners between the ages of 7 and 12 who represent a huge buying demographic. This information is not lost on Disney and the creators of television programs who feature music geared to this burgeoning demographic.

Country music was flying in a huge bubble back in the '90s that subsequently burst, leaving many palatial offices vacant along Music Row. The radio market remains huge, however, and the current crop of new country stars, raised on rock, is capable of generating enthusiastic live audiences for their concerts.

Praise-based music, contemporary Christian and Christian rock, are two genres that are experiencing enormous growth. Dance music, more popular in the urban centers in the U.S., maintains enormous influence in Europe and the U.K.

The New Music Entrepreneurs

Sometimes it seems like everyone has entered the music business. You can't go for a cup of coffee at Starbucks without seeing the latest CD for sale by this caffeinated conglomerate. The success of Ray Charles' *Genius Loves Company* was due in no small part to 1.6 million in sales at the coffee counter. Putumayo Records was founded when a clothing store in New York began putting together world music compilations to play for shoppers.

Soon, customers were begging to purchase copies of the music, giving birth to a profitable record label.

There are many examples of music creators who have turned a handsome profit by following their passions, often far from the beaten track, and I'd like to share some of their experiences with you.

Music for Kids

Music has always been a part of Mae Robertson's life. As an educator in New York who holds a masters degree in Early Childhood Development and Education, she often used music to calm her students. After the birth of her first child, Mae left teaching and opened a successful chain of natural-fiber clothing stores in Westchester County, New York. One night, her friend Don Jackson overheard her singing the traditional folk song "The Water is Wide" while rocking her baby to sleep. When he suggested that Mae record an album of traditional songs geared for families, a new career path was revealed.

Her debut, *All Through the Night,* struck a resonant chord in a public eager for positive, family-oriented music. Since Mae had never promoted a record before, she wasn't aware she was breaking any rules when, with winning enthusiasm, she would naïvely call magazine and newspaper editors and say, "You're going to review it, aren't you?" Surprisingly, they did, and the initial CD sold over 10,000 copies in its first year. Eventually, Mae Robertson sold her clothing stores and dedicated herself to her new career, founding a record label called Lyric Partners.

At the center of an extensive network of significant songwriters, Mae began championing them with the founding of "The Troubadour Series," an ongoing concert program now in its fourth season featuring a slate of nationally touring acoustic artists. Staged at the WorkPlay Theatre in Birmingham, Alabama, these performances are intimate experiences for all fans of the singer/songwriter genre.

Whether she's singing sweet lullabies for children or creating sophisticated words for adults, Mae Robertson's personal vision is the mortar in her artistry. "I want listeners to get lost in the songs with me. Through the beauty of the melodies and the truth in the lyrics, I want to give back dreams."

Soundtrack to a Fast Track

Anytime music is played in any environment—a supermarket, a mall, a gym, onboard an aircraft—someone has made a conscious decision to select it. Major record labels are very hip to this: They purchase spots for their artists on domestic and international flights, in clothing stores, and in movie theaters. The best part of this trend is that it's given the consumer more occasions to hear music, and it's given those who program music—like myself and the companies I work for—more gigs. Corporations are also well aware of the power of music to positively affect buyers, and they use it in a variety of methods far more sophisticated than the simple jingles of the past.

In 1997, the year of its founding, all of Disc Marketing's employees could have fit neatly into one compact car. Today, the Pasadena, California–based music and new media marketing company has over 60 employees housed in a lavishly refurbished Old Pasadena, California, firehouse. The location inspired the name of the adjoining studio, Firehouse Recording, the West Coast's largest ProTools facility.

Tena Clark, a gold and platinum songwriter and record producer, founded the company that now dominates its niche. Through audio, video, new media, print media, and especially music, Disc Marketing (now DMI Networks) deploys ingenious methods for companies to enhance and promote corporate branding and for marketing products to consumers through customized CDs, enhanced CD-ROMs, and CD packages.

In her company's first month of operation, Clark landed a deal with American retail icon Sears, Roebuck & Co. It was just the beginning; Disc Marketing has since created strategic music and entertainment partnerships with the most recognizable corporate brand names in the world, including Coca-Cola, United Airlines, Toyota, Condé Naste, General Mills, Target, Victoria's Secret, Proctor & Gamble, Princess Cruises, and Mrs. Field's Cookies. In 1998, Disc Marketing secured an unprecedented contract to produce all in-flight audio entertainment for United Airlines, now enjoyed by over 19 million monthly travelers worldwide. The company also provides in-flight audio entertainment on the presidential and vice presidential planes, Air Force 1 and 2, United's domestic carrier, Ted, and Regal Cinemedia.

As Disc Marketing continues to expand, new divisions (including a record company and a music library) enable new campaigns, new clients, and new technologies. However, music is still the company's most treasured resource. Tena Clark recently produced the Grammy-nominated album *Church: Songs of Soul and Inspiration* with Patti Labelle, Chaka Kahn, and Dr. Maya Angelou, plus Dionne Warwick's first ever Christmas album. "First and foremost in my heart I'm a songwriter," confirms Clark. It may have all begun with a song, but eight short years later Tena Clark and Disc Marketing are orchestrating a global chorus of commerce, art, and vision.

Internet Notions

As well-noted in all quarters, the rise of technology and the digital transmission of music have radically changed the industry as we know it. The Internet now makes it possible to find a worldwide market for music. Theoretically, an independent artist can have the same online leverage as a major pop act.

Hard-disc based recording systems, notably the industry standard ProTools, make it possible to record a seamless CD in the sonic solace of a spare bedroom and, in theory, to make it available via the Internet and send it out digitally without ever having to leave the house.

According to platinum producer Glen Ballard (Dave Matthews Band, No Doubt, Alanis Morissette, *Polar Express*), filtering artists is a fine art, and he's not hearing fine artists on the Net. "There have been no hit acts off of the Internet. Not one," he insists. "That whole myth of, 'Just wait, we're going to get all of this great music from out there.' There's not one act that has penetrated. There's no filter. People trying to do what we do, identifying talent—most people aren't really going to be able to do it. That filter is getting removed. You have a lot of mediocre stuff."

Mediocre stuff is right. As a journalist, I receive more than 35 independent CDs and press kits a week—every week. Unless something comes to me qualified, which means I'm expecting it, or I have previous knowledge or a relationship with an artist or his representatives, I have no choice but to ignore them. There's simply too much music to absorb, and I have to save my ears for what I have to listen to. Simply having produced a CD is not enough to qualify an artist for media coverage. Positioning like that cannot be purchased. There has to be outstanding music, a real audience, and an angle.

Back in the days, a manager, a producer, a label— *someone* had to believe in an artist's talents before he proceeded in his career. No longer.

Fish or Fowl?

Definitions need to be assigned whether an artist is independent or simply unsigned. Case in point: The Bellrays from Riverside, California. With a 14-year international career that could be the envy of many a major label act (let alone an independent one), the Bellrays possess onstage charisma, unwavering conviction, and a profound ability to impart this belief to their audiences. But the Bellrays usually don't send out free promo copies of their CDs. Anyone is welcome to attend a show and purchase their music.

It's an uncommon stance in a hype-happy town. "We had to do that because we were dealing with a bunch of idiots," says the Bellrays's Tony Fate. "It was too many condescending phone calls from some A&R guy who thought we were going to jump on his dick because he called us up. This guy read something someone wrote because it was thrown on his desk, opened to that page, and he says, 'Yeah, send me a tape.' Well, why? How many tapes do you get a day? Where did you read about us? What are you going to do with it? 'Well, if you don't want to send me a tape forget it.' Sure, forget it."

Bassist Bob Vennum adds, "We only print up a thousand of these things. If we give away 10 of them it's giving away money." And singer Lisa Kekaula continues. "The album is our baby. It's not some promotional tool for the band. It's a labor of love, hurt, pain. And if I'm giving it away you better be worthy of it." But as Fate reveals, the band is certainly open to the right kinds of relationships. "The real people are out there. We set up the net, leave the holes for them to trickle in, and then talk to people who have a plan, who really like the music. We will talk to anyone with an open mind and a brain—at least an intelligent line. But we're not getting a free ride, so why should anybody else? Why should we let somebody who has never seen us, [who] probably won't show up, be on a guest list when he's got a budget that will pay for his ass to come? It's not even coming out of his pocket. Why should we give him a CD when we've got people who come to the shows? I'd rather let them in for free and have him sit outside."

When it's time to cross America, The Bellrays are four smart professionals in a white Dodge van. "Like a church van for a small church," explains Kekaula. They have buzzed Austin's SXSW, toured with Nashville Pussy, and shared stages with artists like Wayne Kramer, Rocket From the Crypt, and The Muffs. In addition, Tony Fate designs promo materials, CD jackets, and T-shirts. "I know there are bands who don't worry about those things," says Kekaula. "Those are more the dinosaurs now than the norm. The bands who are getting that permanent height have been on the road, have been handling things on their own." But it comes back to the audience connection. "We've got to have a lot of foot soldiers out there working for us because we don't have publicity money. The reason people know about us is that we've been out there working on it."

Key Networking Strategy for Artists and Bands

Touring locally and regionally is still the best way to get the word out about you, your band, and your music. Success stories come from everywhere: Omaha, Akron, Sacramento. If you can make a strong enough impression in your home market, believe me, the record labels will find you—that's what they're paid to do.

A Mosaic of Mediums

With the well-publicized downturn in CD sales comes a rise in visual mediums that devour music: network and cable television, video games, and independent film. The explosion of film (independent and studio releases), network and cable television, and video games has spawned more outlets for new music than you can shake a Stratocaster at. This is a good thing because for an independent artist or band, having a song featured on a network television show or in a high-profile film delivers much more than just a sync fee and performance income; it is an indelible sign of media credibility.

For emerging artists and bands, having a song in a film or on a television show offers crucial exposure to a key market. The sync fees can help with substantial monies, and back end payments from a performing rights organization (ASCAP, BMI, or SESAC, for example) can represent a considerable sum for songwriters.

What about songs for television? "The expectation is much lower. It's only recently that the song aspect has come in and made it a pop product," states Robert Kraft, chief executive of Fox Music. "Everything is such short-hand. Television is now a vehicle for delivering songs and a demographic."

Marc Ferrari of the Los Angeles–based MasterSource came into music for picture from the standpoint of a musician/recording artist. "I got into it semi-accidentally," he admits. "I was a major-label recording artist with Keel. We did five albums, and I had another band on MCA. When the grunge thing happened, suddenly it wasn't hip to be a guy that had success in the '80s."

"I had a song used in a small, straight-to-video film. They ended up using it, giving me a screen credit, and giving me some money, and I was like: 'Wow! How about that?' I hadn't thought about providing music for film and TV up to that time. I started representing my own material, and when I would be asked for something I didn't know how to write, like reggae, country, or rap, I turned to friends of mine. That's how it started: I rep'd my friends."

MasterSource has placed over 1,000 songs in over 50 movies, including *As Good As It Gets, Fight Club, Girl Interrupted,* and *The Sixth Sense.* MasterSource TV credits include *Ally McBeal, Buffy The Vampire Slayer, ER,* and *Friends.*

Ferrari is very proactive in seeking out new talent. "I found a lot of writers through reviews in [Los Angeles–based magazine] *Music Connection*," he offers. "And I took out ads also. I still read every issue, demo and concert reviews, and we find so many talented artists right here in our own backyard. Taxi [the independent A&R company] also. They've found some great things for us."

"I don't want to discourage people from following their dreams and pursuing major record deals," concludes Ferrari, "but with the Internet and everything else, a major label deal isn't the end-all it used to be. Film/TV is growing; we have more channels, shows, and it's more music intensive than ever before."

Networking Strategy for Songwriter/Artists

If you want to venture into the world of music for film and television, create two mixes of your material, one without vocals. This way, if a scene calls for music under the dialogue, you have an option.

Radio Is Our Salvation

Major radio has never been amenable to independent or emerging artists. Back in the early days of rock 'n' roll, a labyrinthine system of payola was in place to assure that only select records would be played on radio. The limitations are imposed today by the consolidation of the airwaves by one monolithic corporation, Clear Channel. The airwaves are free and belong to the people, but they are severely regulated by federal decrees and the FCC.

Fact: Radio is an integral component to expose new artists to fans and to uplift local acts to regional and national levels. Accordingly, it is extremely difficult to obtain significant airplay for independent artists. Successful radio promotion revolves around making and managing relationships—who you know and how you know them, making the right contacts, presenting the right pitch, and designing the best spin to convince a station that it should be playing your music. Radio promotion is, therefore, an art that demands a certain style that most artists neither have nor desire to cultivate.

True, specific artists from Fugazi to Phish have achieved monumental record sales without radio, but they are the exceptions. And you probably can't do it alone: Radio is an area where you will need to enroll the assistance of an expert, someone other than you or your manager who is specifically responsible for radio promotion. Therefore, it may be time to hire an independent radio promotion company.

"The best way to get some interest on an indie release is still to have one real success story in one market. There are still a lot of labels, particularly Universal and Atlantic, who are always checking BDS and SoundScan, looking for potential pickups," says Sean Ross, VP of music and programming, Edison Media Research (and former editor in chief of *Billboard's* radio magazine, *Airplay Monitor.* "Even 20 spins for a week or two at one chart reporting station will at least get your record listened to by somebody in major label A&R. At the outset, you're better off building your base in one market and staying in touch with the gatekeepers in that market yourself."

"In the absence of an organic story, what you're probably going to get by putting promoters on a record is the airplay that a given promoter can guarantee on any record at stations where he has a good enough relationship to get anything on the air. That's enough to put some spins on the board, perhaps [and probably in overnights]; probably not enough to propel a record to any significant activity," says Ross.

It is generally acknowledged that radio promotion should be aligned with other career moves, merchandising, and touring. Common sense might dictate that an artist doesn't need a promoter if the record is not going to be distributed in some way; otherwise, the listening audience cannot buy the record, defeating the entire purpose of generating airplay. But radio promoter Bryan Farrish believes that having CDs in conventional stores is irrelevant. "We advise people to forget brick and mortar and only sell during their gigs," says Farrish. "Getting into a physical store is too much work for the amount you sell. You'll do more at one good gig than a year of distribution. Go out, do some shows, sell ten CDs, five T-shirts, pocket the cash plus whatever the gig pays you. People reading this might think, 'If I do radio I need to be in stores.' They're trying to emulate how a label works. There are some things you don't want to emulate."

Joel Denver, president of All Access Promotions, has a background as an on-air personality, a music director, and an editor at *R&R*, and he agrees. "It's terrible to go out, garner airplay, and spend all of that time and effort and not have distribution. If you don't have it, you're not going to sell anything, especially at the brick and mortar level. It's also important to have a good-looking Web site, not a lot of bells and whistles, but something that's clean and operates well. Keep it simple stupid, make sure audiences can find the songs. If you're going to sell them, make them payable through credit card or PayPal. The idea is to make it a good experience for the person visiting the site and listening to the music."

With the consolidation of major radio and the advent of Clear Channel ownership, it might seem that the opportunities for airplay for indie artists are evaporating. Bryan Farrish doesn't see it that way. "The consolidation is a moot point for everyone reading this. It's not going to affect anyone. These stations were never accessible. It's not like something just changed. Thirty years ago [indie artists] wouldn't be getting on the station."

Joel Denver also sees the glass as half full. "I think there's an abundant amount of opportunity out there because the consolidation of major labels provides great opportunities for smaller labels to pitch their product and send the music out via Internet. Although a lot of program directors are playing it safe, there are also plenty out there who want to play new things."

Test shows are key to marketing new acts to radio, explains Farrish. "Many markets have something like 'The Indie Hour' where they play only independent music." Again, these program and music directors have to be reached, sent the music, and the communication followed up on, something in which an indie radio promoter excels. "They have to be reached on the phone, and it's more difficult than at college. You can maybe expect only one or two spins, but you can get on the big stations. And there are charts for those shows."

The relationships that a qualified independent promoter can bring with him are ultimately of supreme value. It's also up to an artist or band to foster and maintain these alliances. Joel Denver shares this example. "I was a music director for a lot of years, so I had dealings with promoters. I remember as a program director staging concerts, needing a band to fill, and having a relationship with a band in town, so I got them some cartage money, a per diem, and had them open the show. If you can cultivate a relationship with a band and the band goes on to be something, that's the shit. You've got to feel good about helping the band, and they'll be good to you. The door has to swing both ways; when you work with a local band it should be win-win."

Satellite, Public, and Internet Radio

Satellite radio may change all of this. Instead of advertising, subscribers pay a fee for unlimited listening to channels that occupy niches and have specialized programming—world music, hard-core punk, Hawaiian music—every conceivable style.

Artist Patti Witten has experienced the successful power of indie promotion. " I think the future for AAA DIY artists like myself is with public/community radio stations whose mainstay is NPR and PRI programming.

It's the right demographic, and you can reach the listeners who seek alternatives to McClear Channel and that ilk. We want to be heard on *World Cafe* and *Sounds Eclectic* and *Weekend Edition*. Sales spikes are huge after features on NPR, especially if you have a presence on Amazon or the digital download sites. Satellite stations are also a good market for us. Indie promoters who specialize and succeed in these markets will find themselves flooded with queries from DIY-ers like myself."

In the major metropolitan center, public radio is a proven taste maker. Here on the West coast we have a station, KCRW, that reaches a relatively small radio audience. However, the audience it reaches is what test marketers refer to as "multipliers"—listeners who can hear a song or an artist and spread the word or take the artist to the next level, such as film directors, music supervisors, and journalists. This tiny station based in a city college in Santa Monica can influence the music heard by billions of listeners in movies and television shows worldwide. Through streaming Internet radio, a syndicated show, *Sounds Eclectic*, a CD compilation by the same name, and the station's sponsorship of events in Los Angeles, San Francisco, and New York, KCRW's image belies its origins in the basement of Santa Monica City College. In the City of Angels, eye-popping big screen ads in Laemelle movie theaters advertise to the cinema-going avant-garde. The policy at KCRW is proudly open door. Music director Nic Harcourt estimates that the station receives maybe 400 CDs per week, and although only a tiny fraction of them ever make it to air, literally everything that comes in is heard.

chris and thomas: Acoustic Essence

Returning from a weekend in Joshua Tree, singer/song-writer duo chris and thomas were greeted by multiple phone messages from excited friends who had heard one of their songs on-air on KCRW-FM. It was news to the pair, whose EP, *The Vista Street Sessions*, was passed on by a mutual friend to the station's music director, Nic Harcourt. The influential DJ programmed it on his show, eventually included it on NPR's syndicated *Sounds Eclectic*, and introduced a national audience to the rustic realness of chris and thomas.

Chris Anderson from Memphis, Tennessee, and Thomas Hien from Munich, Germany, are connected via a trans-Atlantic bond. Island hopping in Greece, Anderson, soon to be a student at the Liverpool Institute for Performing Arts (LIPA) in England, first met a friend of Hien's who connected the two long distance. Eventually, Hien came to visit. Anderson recounts his initial sighting of his future partner in the Liverpool train station "... with a cowboy hat, a John Lennon pinstriped beige and blue suit, python skin boots, sunglasses, and a big metal briefcase."

In time, Hien too was enrolled in LIPA, where he lived with Anderson and a group of student musicians. chris and thomas discovered their shared affinity for the English folk music of John Renbourn, Sandy Denny, and Bert Jansch, but their first major co-venture was multimedia. Teaming up with a local art maven, they devised *Cook Au Van*, whereby they would tool across Europe in a truck converted into a cooking/eating space, invite celebrities like Bill Drummond from KLF and Jarvis Cocker from Pulp onboard to create dinners and videotape the proceedings. Anderson, who was behind the camera, stayed in England to edit and shop the project.

Meanwhile, Hien relocated to Los Angeles, where he knocked around the commercial songwriting scene while Anderson attended art school in Devon, England. Eventually the two reconvened, this time in Hollywood. "For a year we locked ourselves in the house writing and playing—a great year of being creative," reminisces Hien. To document their songs and prepare arrangements, they recorded live with guitars, banjo, mandolin, and the occasional creaking kitchen chair. When singer/songwriter Alexi Murdoch heard these homespun sounds, he invited chris and thomas to open his show at the hip Hollywood venue, the Hotel Cafe.

Having never performed live as a duo, chris and thomas prepared by playing an open mic at an L.A. club. They actually took their own mic, a single AKG condenser, and gathered around it like some modern-day Carter Family, with no additional amplification. The simple presentation underscored the honesty of the songs. Recalls Hien, "We thought the audience would hate it because it's vulnerable music. We got done and it was really quiet, then huge applause. After that we were 'Wow, man!'" Naturalness remains the duo's most thematic through line. "That's what it seems to be about," confers Anderson. "It feels like the music doesn't belong to us—it's almost automatic."

Boosted by the Alexi Murdoch show, and aided by Harcourt's continued airing of their music on KCRW, chris and thomas were in demand as they presented their unadorned art to a growing audience. "For the first two months we didn't book any gigs," notes Anderson. "They called us." They have since signed with major management and are fielding multiple label offers for a first full-length album. They also have placed a song in a documentary set to screen in 90 European cities.

It was the same friend of Hien's whom Anderson met on the Greek island of Mykonos who passed chris and thomas' CD to Nic Harcourt. Serendipity, perhaps, but the success of the duo is testimony that music illuminated by purity and conviction is the most appealing sound of all. *The Vista Street Sessions* is a rare gem of exquisite song craft, intimate, understated performances, and the magical blend of two singers breathing together as one voice. "The music is like our friendship," says Chris. "Effortless," affirms Thomas.

Music Publishing: The Way In

Songwriters are no doubt familiar with the term, "No unsolicited material." The best way to make contact with a publisher, or anyone else in this industry for that matter, is direct referral by an attorney, another songwriter, or a representative of ASCAP, BMI, or SESAC. Two key songwriting events mentioned elsewhere in this book, the West Coast Songwriters Association Conference and the Durango Songwriters Expo, present unprecedented opportunities in comfortable, supportive environments.

A music publisher's willingness to connect with songwriters in controlled situations does not mean that he or she may be pitched to at will. Before contacting any company you should first know what types of music they publish, recent credits, where their strengths lie, what they listen for, and whether they're accepting material in order to determine if you might fit in.

It is important to understand songwriting/publishing terminology, to know what a sync license and a mechanical are, what constitutes a copyright, and the meaning of a reversion clause. Be aware that if you declare to a publisher that you want to "sell your songs," you've just given yourself away as an amateur. Songs are *never* sold, they are published, covered, or collected. The days of "selling songs," thankfully, ended decades ago. (You can educate yourself about the business by reading *Music, Money and Success* by Jeff and Todd Brabec and *The Craft & Business of Songwriting* by John Braheny.)

The bigger publishers generally deal with artists who are already signed to major record deals. If they sign songwriters, they are most interested in writer/producers, especially those who have already attained cuts on their own. Having a publishing deal will make you more desirable as a collaborator, and publishers often make co-writing matches. Even if you're signed to a major publisher, you'll still be expected to hustle up outlets for your songs through your own contacts. The most viable outlets for new songs are film and television.

Networking Strategy for Songwriters

The days of the unattached writer of a single song are long over. Songwriting is a political proposition. If you look at the Billboard charts, you'll observe that virtually all of the songs in top positions are co-written. But the right music publisher is an integral part of songwriting success—proof that someone believes in you and your songs.

_____

Major and Indie Labels

Enthusiasm is a wonderful quality, but imagine running into a friend who has a band and hearing him proclaim the following: "Hey man, come and check out our gig. Capitol Records is comin' down!" Interesting notion, that. Is the entire Capitol Tower coming down? If so, there won't be room for anyone else in the club. The reality is this: An *individual* is coming down to hear the band, and he's currently *employed* by Capitol Records. But guess what? He may not be there next week.

Steady employment in the music business is a volatile proposition. Therefore it's imperative to comprehend this credo: Your relationships should never be with companies, rather your relationships should be with the individuals working in the companies.

I've known many artists who were championed by an A&R executive who signed them to his company. Six months later, when he'd exited the company, the artist was orphaned, with no champion, no advocate. This can lead to a project being "shelved" and never released. At this point, the artist has no choice but to either sit out the contract or repay any advances and recording costs—a very expensive proposition.

But as I've stated before in this book, change is good. For example, the A&R person who is interested in you will probably be moving on to a better position at another company, and now you'll have a contact there. So it may be better all around.

The dominance of major labels is clearly coming to a conclusion. Indie labels—freethinking companies often started on a shoestring and propelled forward by the strength of the music—are at the creative center. These fledgling firms' partnerships with international power-houses complete the circle. Like the great companies of the past—Atlantic, Vanguard, Asylum, Motown—power is being returned on the strength of the music.

Music Biz Marionettes: Who Pulls the Strings?

As infants squalling away in our cribs, mommy comes in, picks us up, and makes everything OK. As adults, we learn to solve our own problems, create our own realities, and quell our sobbing (maybe). Some music business aspirants never move beyond the infantile phase in their thinking, performing in substandard backwater venues, recording endless demos, and imagining that somehow, somewhere, some powerful music industry executive will sweep down, lift them up, and fly them into the stratospheres of fame.

The mythologies of show business are rich with such enticing tales, but they're fictional. In this era, any-one hoping to get a foothold in the multi-billion dollar record business has to prove themselves—locally, region-ally, or internationally—with compelling music and an undeniable career trajectory.

This is equally true for aspiring record company, management, or music publishing executives. No one comes from nowhere. There is a direct through line to the energetic college student who books shows for her university, the tireless volunteer with a local songwriter organization, the band who will drive 12 hours to per-form a 20-minute opening slot, the intern who takes initiative, and the artist who won't wait for a venue to call back. They will create their own success.

I recently helped a college student acquaintance of mine land an intern gig at a record company. After the second week, he called me complaining that he'd not yet done anything even remotely musical, but had only carried boxes around. "And what's in those boxes?" I queried. Hey, no one starts at the top.

The late composer Henry Mancini was once quoted as advising, "Don't be in the music business. Be a music business." If you've sold only one CD at your gig… Congratulations, you're in.

Validation

Art validates its creator. Many times, aspiring and needy recording artists or songwriters will make contact with the industry simply because they need to be heard. Often, they are not even pursuing a real music business career, per se, but they have wrestled some musical creation out of the depths of their psyche, and they want someone else to hear it. It's like a sonic mirror, and they need the gratification of reflection.

If someone wants to spend money to try to get into the music business, believe me, someone will be there to take it. It doesn't matter how much you spend, however; if you don't have the goods, you won't progress any further. I've watched while artists and their supporters have given immeasurable sums of money to demo submission services, so-called music business insiders, questionable lawyers, and over-billing public relations firms. None of these dollars spent did any good—except, of course, for the recipient's bank account. You cannot buy your way into this business.

American Idolization

I was in England a few years back when I took note of the television show *Pop Idols*, featuring a competition between singers with the winner determined by the votes of an immense television audience. My students at LIPA—hipper than hip musicians—despised the concept, but I was mesmerized by the potential cross-marketing that could be achieved. I was not surprised, then, when a U.S. version, *American Idol*, became a smash hit. These types of shows are nothing new. *Major Bowles Amateur Hour* was the *American Idol* of its day, and *Star Search* also had its audience in the '80s.

From an entertainment standpoint, these shows are a hoot and, I confess, a guilty pleasure for me as well. The buffoonery aspect is the first hook. In the preliminary round, audiences like to see someone act dumber than they do. In the U.K., it was explained to me, audiences always root for the underdog—the singer with the speech impediment; a vocalist who doesn't have the same svelte shape as the others. This is true to a degree in the U.S. as well. The overweight teddy bear, the single mother, and the nerd turned glamour boy have all found fame.

Such shows have given voice to the screaming school of vocal histrionics, where every note sung is divided into interminable syllables and wrung dry. I was in Ohio watching the *American Idol* show at my parents' house when my mother passed through the room and observed a shrieking contestant competing in the finals. "I don't know if she's good," commented my mother, "but she sure is loud."

This show embodies multiple layers of classic entertainment. It's funny, with its humor built on cruelty and laughing not with but at those deluded into thinking they have talent at the early auditions. Then there is the pathos of "rags-to-riches" stories, with Cinderella-like transformations of the winning contestants from geeks to gods and goddesses. And not least, the audience participation and emotional connections through the voting phone-ins.

Truth is, all of those who have found fame on this show—with the notable exception of one William Hung—have been working at their craft for most of their young lives. They are well-seasoned professionals with a fanatical devotion to their craft and unerring instincts toward their art.

As alluring a fantasy as it may seem, no one comes from nowhere. Britney Spears, Christina Aguilera, and Justin Timberlake were all Mouseketeers as children. They grew up in the business. This is a through line for those who are called to be entertainers, musicians, and songwriters. In my experience, it is not a choice, but a calling—the undeniable need for expression through music and performance, hard-wired into your very being and the dominant thread in the fabric of your existence. Your identity, not something that happens between 8:00 and 9:00 P.M. on your television.

Summary

CD sales are simply one facet of an emerging multi-platform media market. If music were a science, it would be scrutinized, analyzed, and dominated by corporations. Nothing succeeds like the sound of honest music, and we succeed only when we're honest with ourselves, others, and most of all, our medium.

CHAPTER 3

Personalities Plus

This chapter examines the importance of personalities. I'll suggest specific ways to gauge your strengths and possible weaknesses. I'll begin with 10 shared attributes of successful music biz practitioners.

Ten Successful Attributes of Music Biz Professionals

1. **Talent**
    As I explained in the Introduction to this book, every persuasive trick in the book won't help you if you do not have the goods. We all have talent, and some incredibly lucky people are born with it, but for most of us it's a lifelong pursuit to develop it. And not just musical talent either—it may be a talent for sales, for convincing others, for offering support and clarity.

2   **Training and Education**
    For singers, songwriters, and band members, this should be fairly self evident. You will always benefit from lessons

and on-the-job experiences, especially by hanging out with those who are more proficient than you. If you're more inclined to the business side of things, the same creed applies. Reading about the business you're in should be the first fundamental rule. I was on a panel recently at an L.A. college with a senior member of the A&R staff of a major record label. "How many of you read *Billboard* every week?" he queried the room. When a paltry third of those in attendance raised their hands, he noted, "So, you want to be in the music business, but you don't read the publication every single executive reads?"

Billboard, e-mail journals, and *Hits!* magazine are all available online. If you don't have a computer, use the one at your local library. You can browse your library's magazines, too, or simply go to your local Borders or Barnes & Noble bookstore and stand at the magazine counter and read until they ask you to leave. By educating yourself over a period of time, you'll begin to draw a correlation between executives and events and to demystify this multi-level, interconnected business.

Universities and colleges offer classes in the music business, although, as I often tell my students, I didn't have this advantage during my educational years. We formed bands, bought vans, went on the road, and moved to Nashville, New York, and L.A. For me, teaching at a learning environment like The Liverpool Institute for Performing Arts in the U.K. or Cal Poly Pomona in Southern California is a welcome affirmation that, yes, this is a real academic pursuit. As always, the real value of any situation is in the human contacts you make.

3. **A Big Personality**
Personality bears a resemblance to talent in that some of us are born with it, and others take longer to develop it. The entertainment business is absolutely filled with individuals with large personalities—quirky, offbeat, or entertaining. What we relegate to the domain of the personal is strongly influenced by levels of confidence. A strong personality often mirrors a high degree of self-confidence.

It's not necessary to enter a room like a bull charging into a ring, to buttonhole everyone in attendance, and to dominate the proceedings, but a winning personality is the ability to draw others to you.

4. **A Positive Outlook**
I've believe in the ability of positive people to determine the outcome of their own destinies through the strength of their convictions and their winning attitudes. I'll reiterate my belief here: Positive thoughts and energies attract positive results.

5. **Enthusiasm**
This is not simply bluster and hype, but the honest result of having something to share with others that you feel is absolutely essential.

Much of my telephone time as a journalist is taken up in speaking with publicists who call me with pitches for their clients. I can tell when the enthusiasm is real and when it's simply an hourly billing. It's not so much in their words, but in the intentions and energies behind them. Music people have a sixth sense for this. In some instances a publicist will ask me to listen to their client with the promise that "This music will absolutely affect you." Hopefully, that's true, because if the music doesn't affect me, this ploy won't work again.

6. **Entertainment Value**

If you're in the entertainment business, doesn't it make sense that you must also provide entertainment for those with whom you speak and interact? I shared this thought on a panel at a recent songwriter confab and was greeted with some derision by a fellow panelist (somewhat of a curmudgeon, I might add). I was wearing an iridescent green shirt and multi-colored Mardi Gras beads, acquired at a local wine tasting event. But my outfit made a point, and for the remainder of that day, I was highly identifiable to anyone who wanted to seek me out.

Entertainment is not limited to the in-person effect. In Chapter 6, "Telephone and E-Mail," I talk about the importance of "Giving Good Phone." In our lives and businesses, as we transmit the power of entertainment, we must have our own intrinsic performance value. It's called playing the role—it's what a lawyer does in a courtroom, what determines a dynamic minister in a pulpit, what makes a police officer a figure of authority.

7. **Desire and Determination**

I put desire and determination together because I believe they're interrelated. Desire is a wish, a craving, and a longing, while determination is a firmness of purpose, will, and resolve. My hair-cutter, Armando, is full of intriguing insights. Born and raised in Los Angeles, he recently observed, "It takes you guys from these weird small towns to come out to Hollywood and kick ass." I found this interesting on a number of levels, and he's right. There does seem to be a disproportionate number of success stories that emanate from transplants from the middle of the country.

When I was a kid, I resented the fact that I had been born in the middle of Ohio. But I realize now that it was this very fact that helped provide the determination and focus of my career. Because we didn't have a music and art scene, my friends and I invented one. We created our own venues for music and performance. It was these inclinations that bonded us to each other. Yes, we were viewed as outsiders, but this alienation found an outlet through art.

Just getting out of Lima, Ohio, was my beginning, when I understood that I couldn't make a living there, that I would have to leave the sanctuary of a loving family, to fly from the nest, to live in poverty in strange cities and on the road. Leaving home propelled me and fueled me with the energy I have to this day. Rarely is anyone lucky enough to stay in a comfort zone, especially at the beginning of a career.

8. Commitment and Timing

People sometimes say, "If I don't make it in a year, I'm going to do something different." Oh boy. What do you think will happen to the career of someone who states an objective constructed around time constraints? Time is relative, flexible, on a continuum. In our careers, although we can invent goals and look toward milestones, attempting to align ourselves to a time grid is a self-defeating proposition.

As I stated at the onset of this book, we cannot *make* things happen, we can only put ourselves in the position *where* things can happen. This may take years, decades, or even the time of an entire career. Music, and the life we live creating and working with it, chooses us. If we give ourselves an out, that dreaded "something to fall back on," we're negating and undermining our determination. Sure, we might have to step back, access the situation, open our eyes to new possibilities, and create variations on a theme. But if our commitment is not total, we can't expect others' reactions to our art and work to be 100 percent, either.

9. **Create Your Own Opportunities**
   You will not be spoon fed in the music business. This I can guarantee you: The only person who can elevate you is you. Those who walk a successful career path have trained themselves to do so. Virtually every powerful manager, agent, or promoter in the business began on very humble ground, promoting local shows, handling beginning artists, booking high schools, colleges, or local shows.

   Don't say "I'm thinking about…," "I'm considering…," "I'm wondering…." No. Those of us who succeed in the music business have no other options. It's who we are. Do it now, always, forever.

10. **Understand When to Permit Emotion to Overtake Logic**
    "My college professor told me that I have a better chance of winning the lottery than getting a record deal," admitted a dejected music business student. Oh great, just what we need, another cynical academic deflating the dreams of a student. Shame on the teacher for spouting this drivel. What if he'd said this to Bruce Springsteen, Michael Stipe, or Andre 3000 and Big Boi from OutKast? We're talking apples and oranges; there is simply no relationship between winning a game of chance and

building a career to the point where a major record label would be interested in an artist.

As discussed throughout this book, a major-label deal may not even be the best road for an enterprising creative artist, particularly at this historic time, when independent artists are emerging as new power brokers.

Speaking of record deals, a friend of mine recently had two labels regularly coming to his shows, interested in signing him. He attempted to play the two companies against each other, to up the ante so to speak, and ended up alienating both labels. He was attempting to determine which company to sign with based on his analytical mind, breaking down advances, percentages, and other contract details, when he should have been paying attention to the emotional commitment offered by an earnest A&R man who genuinely believed in the power of his music.

Lawyers and managers are paid well to be analytical. Understanding the business is, of course, a prerequisite to being in it, but don't permit logic to derail your heart and soul. Because if you were truly logical and normal, you wouldn't even be in the music business, would you?

Negative Notions

We know them all too well: naysayers, pessimists, prophets of doom and gloom. "A&R people wouldn't know a good song if it bit 'em on the butt" or, "The record companies are crooks and gangsters," or, "Commercial music is such bullshit." Negativity is a tellingly potent force. It often manifests itself in character traits including self-doubt, lack of self-worth, and low self-esteem. It is also highly contagious. If we allow them, negative people have the power to deflate us, to bring us down to their level—in short, to make us feel bad. As a longtime player, I bristle when I hear put-downs of the music industry from those who want to enter into it telling me that the business to which I've devoted the majority of my life is a sham, a con, a dark netherworld of shady characters and disreputable operators. I'm also keenly aware that this can be a self-defense mechanism used by those who doubt their own abilities. After all, why bother to succeed in an industry that's such a shithouse? They're projecting their own sense of doom on an entire business.

In music, as in life, optimists are much more successful in reaching career heights. Much of this has to do with the power of self-fulfilling prophecy—those who expect to succeed will do so. There is an attendant human factor, too: Positive energy attracts positivity, and positive people attract others to them.

This is, of course, essential in a business built on buzz, fueled by the energy and the eternal promise of "the next big thing." Savvy business people clamber to get on a train that's already up and rolling. Since music and the businesses it supports are interactive, it is our quest to attach ourselves to others in the same service of success.

There is even scientific evidence proving that optimists live longer, have more productive lives, experience less illness (mental and physical), and achieve far more than pessimists, because an optimistic frame of mind modulates the nervous system. A study of first-year law students at UCLA showed that optimists had higher levels of disease-fighting killer cells in their blood than did pessimists.

So, in planning your course of action, keep in mind that it will always be easier to change the way we think about the world than to change the world itself.

The Put Down

I was asked to critique a self-penned bio for a new acoustic duo that included the phrase "In this age of negligible, overproduced music." I advised them to edit this line out since it was clear they'd superimposed their own prejudices and opinions into a piece that should have been uplifting and about their music, making it shine in comparison to others. Also, they might be pitching themselves to the very executives who had signed, produced, or promoted that "negligible, overproduced music."

Passing judgment on music is a dicey proposition. When my students in music schools make grave pronouncements based on their prejudices, I gently remind them that musicians aren't the ones buying records—it's the general public. Pop music, specifically, seems to raise their hackles (and of course the more it sells, the more my students detest it). My British students detest American country. Sure, certain styles of music speak to us and others don't, but as music people it's essential to be open to all forms of expression. If you hear a form of music that's unfamiliar, begin analyzing it. What are its reference points? What do the performers look like?

51

What is their audience? What are the other connecting points—for example, the fashion, politics, or lifestyles?

Over roughly two decades, hip-hop music (with estimated annual CD sales of $2.8 billion) and its surrounding culture, have become an indomitable force. On occasion, I've heard harsh judgments made on rap and hip-hop—"That's not music," being one of the kinder pronouncements. Judgments such as these serve only to diminish my opinion of the speaker. It also makes me wonder if they dislike black music or black people. I recall the "Disco Sucks" craze of the late '70s. Did those who were burning their Donna Summer records hate the relentless beat, or did they dislike those who were dancing to it in the discos?

Whether it is teen pop or Tuvan throat-singing, I contend that there is something to be learned from every form of music. What is often being projected by harsh and negative judgments is a closed mind and jealousy. If someone says to me, "I hate rap music," I am appalled that they can put the words "hate" and "music" into one sentence. This is not an individual with whom I would choose to work.

Negative to Positive

In order to break through, it's essential to eliminate the negative people in your life. (OK, maybe they are members of your family, or even your spouse or partner, in which case you must acknowledge, and then eliminate, their negative influence over you.) As children we are programmed in very specific, often unintentional, ways by our families. To reconfigure our patterns of thought, it is first essential to identify the traits in ourselves that amplify negativity.

I was once working in a music industry position that required interaction with a large staff. One of the key employees would invariably attend planning meetings with a scowl on his face and would begin every sentence with the phrase "The problem with that is…." Whether we were planning a show, a conference, a publication, or an event, he was the one dark cloud hovering over the conference table, always predicting the dire outcome of events that had not yet transpired. I remember him rushing backstage after one of our shows and remarking, "Great show; the only complaint I've heard so far…" before I stopped him. He was taken aback. "You don't want to hear criticism?" he asked. "Not while the applause is still ringing in the hall," I insisted.

You can probably guess the outcome of his history at the company. When cutbacks were made and restructuring was announced, he was the first one to be let go. In collaborative relationships, there is a value in having a team member who thinks of potential liabilities, but no one wants to exist under the constant onslaught of relentless negativity. No one wants to hear it.

When I was managing artists, I would sometimes encounter music business colleagues who were intent on tossing their wet blanket over the proceedings. "What's up with the guy you manage?" was often the beginning. I would take note if they didn't call him by name. When I would indicate that we were in preliminary meetings with a specific record label, I would hear, "Oh, that company. They're having a lot of problems over there, aren't they?" Again, simple negativity.

Find Reasons to Feel Good about Yourself

I'm an inveterate list-maker with yearly, monthly, weekly, and daily plans of action. It's the proverbial "small stuff" that often fuels the most vital day-to-day operations. You can do something everyday for your music business career: doing research on the Internet, reading *Billboard* at the library, watching and observing videos, making calls, going out to hear music. When your plans are intentional and charted you have a much better course of action. Check off items that you've accomplished. In addition to having made progressive steps forward in your career, you have also achieved something for yourself, and that's a reason to pat yourself on the back. Remember that your small victories and accomplishments will add up in time.

Use your time effectively; pick your prime time, then prioritize tasks by asking yourself, "Will accomplishing this help me get where I want to be in five or ten years?"

Visualize Your Success

An exercise I once used while teaching at the Liverpool Institute for Performing Arts stands out in my mind. In a room full of students, I asked one young man what he wanted to accomplish in his career. "I'd like to make enough money to buy a house," was his answer. Where would this house be? "On a cottage lane." What were the dimensions of the house? "An upstairs and a downstairs." What color is the door? "A red door." As we went further down the list, suddenly this ephemeral house he was visualizing began to take shape in his mind. He was on his way to moving into it because he'd built it in his imagination.

Network with People You Respect and Observe Their Traits

Throughout this book I've emphasized the value in making others feel good. When I conducted an on-camera interview with legendary R&B powerhouse vocalist, Patti LaBelle, her first words of introduction to me were a compliment on my sport coat as she reached over and felt the sleeve. A small act, to be sure, but one that spoke immeasurably of her interest, and kindness, to others.

I was very fortunate to have come up under the guidance of powerful music business mentors. Respect for others and their feelings is a vital trait. I'm reminded that successful people have their own doubts, fears, and struggles, too, so it's natural that we feel that way as we face the daunting odds of taking our music into the marketplace. The value of aligning yourself with a supportive network of caring friends and colleagues cannot be over-emphasized. Unless you have a crystal ball, you may not know where your contacts will ultimately arrive, but rest assured, if you're around strong, upbeat, positive people, they are likely already on their way to formidable destinations. And hopefully, so are you.

The Smooth Road

This week I moderated a hit songwriter panel in Hollywood at the DIY (Do It Yourself) Convention. It was a formidable panel, assembled by BMI, with my guests including Chad Hugo, one half of the multiple

Grammy Award-winning writing and production duo, The Neptunes.

At the conclusion of our allotted time, we opened the room up to questions from the attendees. One young man strode to the mic and announced, "I'm here to give my CD to Chad Hugo from The Neptunes." Chad explained that because of the legal ramifications, it was not possible for him to accept material.

You're probably familiar with the scenario where an unknown songwriter claims his song was stolen by a famous artist. Undoubtedly, most of these cases have proven to be entirely without merit, but what must be proven in every instance is access. Record labels, recording artists, producers, or songwriters who accept material from an unknown source run the risk of opening themselves up to future legal liability. Of course, the more successful the recipient, the greater the probability that this might occur, and only successful, income generating songs are ever deemed to be "stolen." Hence the famous "No unsolicited material" credo.

But the legal challenges are secondary. The most telling action by this young man was that in his mind he had deduced that the quickest way to the top was via someone who was already there. When I pointed out that he needed to find the *next* Chad Hugo, or Neptunes, or Matrix, or Jimmy Jam and Terry Lewis, he indignantly countered with this proclamation: "It's like a Cadillac. I want the fastest, smoothest ride. That's The Neptunes."

Oh, if it were only that simple. No one can make you famous, sail you in on their considerable coattails, and launch your career for you. Of course, having The

Neptunes craft tracks for you would be amazing. But in a mercantile world, The Neptures reportedly earn hundreds of thousands of dollars for creating a track, and these fees are gladly paid by the record companies. They have their own label, A&R staff, publishers, and managers and are surrounded by an immense support staff. It's not only two songwriter/producers pulling talented artists from a pool and making them stars but an entire creative mechanism.

Myths

It is a fallacy, a myth, and a misconception to think that the quickest way to success is through others who are already there. Since I've interviewed the best-known songwriter/producers in the business, I'll have aspiring songwriters ask me, "Could you give my CD to (insert one) The Matrix, Glen Ballard, Jimmy Jam and Terry Lewis?"

I have to say "No." First off, I understand my role in the pantheon of the music business. If I'm there as a journalist or interviewer, and I suddenly start whipping out demos and press kits, I wouldn't be in this business long, would I? Also, I'd be staking my reputation on the materials I presented.

If you play or present music to anyone of importance, nothing can be left to chance: Your talents have to be undeniable. I've had publicists rave to me about their clients, but when the music arrives it is sub-par. As a result, I will never trust that person's judgment again and would certainly be less likely to listen to anything he sent me in the future. This is not a matter of being cold hearted, but a reality of our business. Time wasted listening to inadequate or badly conceived music is time lost, never to be regained. Plus it's depressing.

Have I ever played anything for any of these luminaries I mentioned? Yes, once. It was a track by a new artist, and it ended up being included in a film. Once. In all these years. It's self protection for the reputation and assurance that anything I present in the future will be of similar, sterling quality.

Reinvention

As talented people, we are often at a distinct disadvantage in recognizing what sets us apart from the crowd. We wake up in the morning, stare at the disheveled image in the mirror, and go about our daily lives of creating magic—literally, conjuring up something from nothing with music and art. It's often too easy to overlook the incredible abilities with which we've been bestowed. Sometimes it takes someone from outside of our sphere to make us realize how gifted and how lucky we really are.

Earlier in the book I referenced my career and its progression through cities, decades, and vocations, with music always at its core. I refer to this evolution as "reinvention," and learning when and how to reinvent has been a prime ingredient in my longevity.

At every stage in our life, our needs are changing. As children aspiring to be musicians and performers, we were probably motivated by the perceived status and glory of the stars we observed in the popular media.

Having a burning need to communicate drives many musicians to become songwriters. Feeling powerless motivates many songwriters to become producers, dissatisfaction with the way the music business is run may inspire a record producer to become a record executive, and so on.

Reinvention works only when there is a natural progression between the steps in the business. I was well aware when it was time for me to move beyond playing in bands and writing songs. Not that I couldn't continue (if I wished), but as the venues repeated, the opportunities dried up, and time ticked away, I knew it was time for a change.

Nothing stays the same—either your career is moving up or it's moving down. I know bands who have stayed their steady course, waiting for a record deal that never comes, who continue to make exactly the same moves, play the same venues, and ultimately burn out their audience. No one wants to go to the same place and do the same things year after year. Human nature requires stimulation.

Same Old Same Old

Allegedly, Albert Einstein said that doing the same thing over and over and expecting a different result is the mark of insanity. There is certainly truth in this statement. The music industry, too, becomes wary over time. Our business is marked by the "newest," "freshest," and "hippest." Artists who aren't perceived to have these adjectives attached to them will suffer over time.

For example, there was a well-known Los Angeles band who had a residency at one of the city's most influential clubs. Even though A&R reps would come and see the group play, after a year the consensus was that if they were so good, why hadn't they been signed?

Here is an interesting reality. It is often easier to sign an artist to a deal if they've already had a deal. In other words, even if they've been dropped, because their credibility has been proven once, an enterprising record label may be more willing to take a change on them than they would on a new, unproven act. Similarly, it is often easier to have a song recorded if there is a history of previous recordings.

We speak of the "herd mentality" in the music industry. If we were creating an invention in the "real world," we would concoct something that no one had ever seen. But in the music business, when a trend connects, there is a rush to duplicate the initial successes, be they shoe-gazing emo rock bands, lithesome pop singers, recently jailed hip-hop felons, or flag-waving country acts. If the public has bought something once, they will buy it over and over again. And herein lies another paradox: Pop music is a savvy combination of what is fresh and what is familiar.

Summary

Discouragement can be a fact of life in all of our endeavors. I've witnessed multitudes of people who can no longer navigate the treacherous currents of the music business and choose to make their lives elsewhere. This is good: It creates more opportunities for the rest of us.

I'm no Einstein, but here's another theory: You can't get out of a business that you're not in. In other words, you're not really in the business if you don't give it your full commitment.

Do you need stability in your life? A steady paycheck? Odds are, you won't have it in the entertainment industry, especially in the early stages of your career. It's a business where not only do you have to walk the path, you also have to clear the brush and pave it as well. That's too much for most normal people.

But then again, you're not "normal," are you? What did your family tell you about making a living in this crazy business? That you need something to fall back on? If you're energetic and goal oriented and can create opportunities for yourself, that is your strongest resource; that is your fallback position.

In his song "Something to Believe In," singer/songwriter Shawn Mullins says

Don't let it pass you by
Someday you'll wake up asking yourself why
You sat there at your desk
Sucking on the corporate breast.

If the music is in your soul, it will show you the path.

CHAPTER 4

True Tales

This chapter examines various true-life scenarios. You'll venture behind the velvet rope to view the underpinnings of the music business and its participants.

The I's Don't Have It

Just prior to presenting a two-hour "Networking in the Music Business" seminar at a popular California music conference, I ran into an old acquaintance in the hallway. Before uttering a single word of greeting, she thrust a flyer promoting her upcoming show into my hands. "I would come see you speak today," she informed me breathlessly, "but you know I've got this networking thing down." Oh good. This meant I could use her (anonymously, of course) as an example in my lecture that afternoon.

The combination of an inflated ego and a sense of insecurity is a volatile combo, one quite common in the entertainment business. For our purposes, let's examine the simple dynamics of conversation. Some people seem to think of communication only on their own terms: What they project, how they come across, how others perceive them. The exact opposite approach is what works best.

Those who begin virtually every sentence with the word "I" are tiresome in any situation. Try beginning any social interaction with a question like, "What new projects have you been working on?" What you're projecting with this query is interest. You've also served the proverbial ball across the imaginary net; when your conversation partner concludes his explanation of recent endeavors, he will in all probability ask you what you've got going on. Now it's your turn.

Making others feel important is a vital communication skill. Honestly listening to what others have to say, asking questions to move the conversation along, offering affirmations like, "It must be wonderful to be realizing this project," all do wonders to impart a warm glow. But you have to be truthful, to honestly care, to make this work.

The Power of "You"

Here's an interesting note on verbal communication. Suppose your friend or romantic partner drops you off at home following a fun day of recreation. You say, "Thanks, I had a really good time." Now examine the emotional impact of that reply compared to the added significance of this variation: 'Thanks, I had a really good time *with you*."

Note the difference? You've connected the emotions of your pleasure to the presence of another person. You've included them in response to you. It's an easy way to give added impact to your declaration, with just the addition of the word "you."

Could'a, Should'a, Would'a

When I was a beginning songwriter and first experiencing industry interest in my songs, I made a common mistake—I talked about something before it happened. My co-writer and I had a song recorded by a major star of the day. I was so thrilled that I told everyone within hearing range about this coup—friends, family, audiences at gigs where I was performing, complete strangers at parties. As time went on, and I encountered these folks again, invariably they would ask me, "So, what's happening with your song?" Time went by, the artist changed producers, labels, and direction, and the song was never released. Meanwhile, I had credibility issues since my big break that I'd trumpeted so proudly went belly-up.

Here's some categorical advice on the subject:

1. As my big brother used to caution me back in Ohio, "Almost doesn't count in anything but horseshoes."

2. Recording artists, particularly in Nashville, think nothing of putting a hundred songs presented by songwriters and publishing companies "on hold." Sure, they may be interested in cutting them, but there is also a theory that they're taking the good songs—those written by other

writers that may otherwise be recorded by their chart competitors—out of circulation.

3. No song is for certain until it's released. Artists typically record more songs than they need for any given project.

4. The calendar of popular music has little relationship to the real world.

5. Artists, films, and television shows can all be dropped, and songs can be replaced up until the last possible second.

6. You've got to have more than one thing going on. Obviously, the more irons you have in the fire, the greater probability of one of them turning red hot.

7. The tired phrase "we're waiting to see" is a dead giveaway that nothing is happening. People who have it going on don't ever wait.

8. Thanking others for your successes projects a welcome sense of humility. For example, "it was an honor to" perform at a benefit, to have a song recorded, to open a show. "We were surrounded by brilliance."

9. Admit when things don't turn out without conveying rancor or bitterness. No one likes a sore loser.

10. Keep in mind that it's not only our successes that endear us to others, it's our willingness to survive the swells of adversity, to persevere, to take the hits and get back up.

12. Always crowing about your the next big thing and having nothing materialize will greatly damage your credibility.

13. Better to be enigmatic and slightly mysterious than to be overblown and pretentious. People who really have it going on don't have to tell you about it, and it is better to exude quiet confidence than project the bellow of a human bullhorn.

It's much better to have someone else speak positively about you than to huff and puff and emit endless clouds of self-serving hype on your own behalf. Given my background in sales and public relations, it is very natural for me to tout the accomplishments and talents of my friends and colleagues. In turn, when I'm out socially, many of my close friends in the business return the favor.

If someone tells me "My band is amazing," I file away this information in a little dumpster dubbed "Hype." Having someone *not* in a band tell me "I saw the most amazing band last night!" intrigues me, especially if I trust that person's judgment. Nothing is more effective in marketing than word of mouth. Having someone else speak on your behalf is much more effective than blowing your own horn. If you honestly believe it and promote your friends, they'll do the same for you provided you've got it going on.

You're It

Tag teams are equally effective in other social situations. In Chapter 5, "Making Contact," I speak about the value of, and the tricks for, remembering names, but of course there are instances when we all forget. If I'm out socially with a music industry tag-team partner, we'll discuss this contingency beforehand. "If I don't introduce you by name in the first 30 seconds, introduce yourself," I'll explain. The unnamed party will then offer his name for all to know.

If you do attend events with others, make sure you share a common agenda. I don't take romantic partners with me to business events. If given the option, I'd rather invite a friend whose social skills I trust and who is a devotee to *Networking Strategies*. One of my close business friends is an executive in the music publishing division at a major Hollywood film studio. His perspective on the business is much more market savvy, more bottom-line dollars and cents, than my often-Quixotic outlook. But between us, we've got it covered, and the contrasts are what make us an effective tag team socially. He also possesses an acerbic sense of humor, doesn't take himself too seriously, and sees the big picture and knows where he fits into it.

Bridges Aflame

I mention this friend for another reason. As he was coming up in the world of music publishing, he was employed by a veteran music publisher who had been in the business for decades and who represented some very lucrative catalogs. My friend worked endless hours, endured the "low man on the totem pole" position, and was not rewarded monetarily for his work since his boss was extraordinarily cheap. He finally left that company on good terms, but he considered writing a letter to the boss, telling him of the indignities he'd suffered—a "kiss-off" letter.

Fortunately, he reconsidered. And a couple of years down the road when the music division of one of the world's largest film studios was looking for an executive, they called the veteran publisher for a recommendation, who referred them to my friend.

Celebrity

As an interviewer and journalist, I often find myself in the presence of the foremost hit makers in American music. Meeting these legends is a consummate thrill, but I can never lose sight of what I need from them: credible interview material.

Earlier this year, I was at the Bel Air home of Quincy Jones for the taping of a video segment commemorating the anniversary of the performing rights organization, ASCAP. Mr. Jones, of course, is one of the most celebrated record producers in history. As the video crew set up in anticipation of his arrival and a maid served veggies, fruit, salsa, and chips (a nice touch), I looked over my notes and thought ahead to what I would say when I was introduced to the pop maestro. Although a number of possible scenarios ran through my head, I realized the interaction would take its own course.

The video producer brought Mr. Jones to the corner of the room where we'd arranged the set and introduced us. I shook Quincy Jones' hand, looked him straight in the eye, and said "Hey man."

"Hey man," responded Quincy Jones.

Amazing. Everything I know and have experienced in the trenches of the music business was distilled down into those two words. I didn't prostrate myself at Mr. Jones' feet, tell him what an inspiration he was and what a profound honor it was to meet him. My instincts commanded me to remain casual and relaxed, mirroring the energy I felt emanating from Mr. Jones.

Living in Los Angeles, where it's not unusual to see Brad Pitt at a local eatery, Ben Affleck in a Porsche on the Santa Monica Freeway, or Beyonce shopping for bling, celebrity is serious business. But my business is music, and I've found that when I interview celebrities, what they enjoy most about my interviews is that I never ask them typical, celebrity-driven questions. I save that for the supermarket tabloids. My only concern for interviews is music and its creation. From Clint Eastwood to Metallica, Queen Latifah to Brian Wilson, I'm reminded of what draws us together as creative people. There is no "Us" and "Them." It's all us.

Ten Strategies for Interacting with Celebrities

Sometime in your career, you will meet people whom you or the media consider celebrities. As always, your instincts will guide you, and your communication skills and level of self-confidence will determine the outcome of this contact. Following are some tips to keep in mind when the opportunity arises to interact with celebrities.

1. Always keep in mind that they're just people, too. Acknowledging their music or contributions is fine; just don't overdo it.

2. Know where to draw the line at being a fan. Make no mistake, celebrities love fans, but they don't work with them—no autographs or photos, please.

3   Respect their physical space and observe their interactions with handlers, managers, publicists, and so on for cues.

4. Don't be presumptuous.

5. Be careful not to age them. Telling a diva of certain years that you listened to her "when you were a little boy" will not endear you to her. Trust me!

6. If you do need to initiate conversation, ask general life questions as opposed to career questions. For example, "Are you in town for the show, or will you have a chance to enjoy the city?"

7. If you know someone in common, this is can be an excellent ice-breaker. This always works well for me. A word of caution, however: Since human relationships are volatile and ever shifting, make sure that the name you drop is of someone with whom the artist still has a good relationship.

8. Don't offer information you haven't been asked for, such as your current projects, your political opinions, or artistic/musical judgments.

9. Never put pressure on a musical celebrity to listen to or look at…*anything.*

10. Keep the doors open. Let them know how much you enjoyed meeting them and that hopefully you'll see them in the future.

How Would I Reach You?

This is fresh to me since it happened last night outside a club in Hollywood. I interviewed a hugely successful songwriter/producer at a monthly event, "The Songwriters Studio." As he left the venue, he was accosted in the foyer by an aspiring singer/songwriter who offered, "I don't want to waste your time, but I'm going to want to contact you about a year from now. How do I get hold of you?"

The hit maker answered, "Dan knows, just ask him," and walked away.

By making me responsible, the hit maker gently deflected the inquiry, but I mention this story for another reason. The aspiring songwriter projected his insecurity with his vague "a year from now" dialogue; therefore, his inquiry served no real purpose other than to foist him in the hit writer's face for a nanosecond. Knowing how to contact someone is one of the arts that must be mastered in our business. It's not the responsibility of the contactee—in this case the hit writer—to offer up his contact information. Finally, it's off-putting and pretentious for a beginning songwriter to assume that this multi-platinum, Grammy Award winning legend would remember him a year from now—let alone want to work with him.

Who Needs You?

· ·

I recently lectured to a music business class at a well-known California college and the next day received the following e-mail.

Dear Dan,

I attended your class last night. You were talking to students afterward and I didn't want to disturb you, so I'm sending this e-mail instead.

All my life I've dreamed of being a lyricist. I know I have what it takes to make my dreams come true. In class you said you're writing for a Web site and that one of the founders is Kenneth "Babyface" Edwards. Would you please give the attached lyrics to him so he can put the music to them?

Thank you,
A Talented Lyricist

Following is my reply:

Dear Talented,

I don't wish to sound cold, but in my opinion Mr. Edwards probably does not need you. Whitney Houston does not need you either. Nor does Celine Dion or Toni Braxton.

Why? First of all, if you are a songwriter who writes lyrics, you need to find collaborators who create music so your songs can exist as a complete unit. But I'm far more concerned about other issues.

Dreams are wonderful things. Indeed, most creative people share the ability to see beyond the mundane limitations of everyday life. Goals are dreams with deadlines. In establishing your career in the music business, you need to understand the marketplace for your material and the realities of it.

It's only when you seize control of your career that you succeed. Find acts and artists who are coming up, who require direction and material. Instead of looking up and fantasizing about Babyface, look on your own level to find the next Babyface, Timbaland, or Diane Warren. Attach yourself to people whose success you can predict; indeed, be one of them yourself.

When you buy into the "overnight success" mythology you set yourself up for disappointment and exploitation. The music business is built on relationships. In my decades in this business, every deal I've seen go down has been the result of a personal contact. It's all about hard work, dedication, perseverance, and people skills. I have never known anyone to start at the top.

Something else bothers me. You were too shy to come up and talk to me after class. I came there to meet you, to offer any advice that I could, to make contact. If you were not assertive enough to make my humble acquaintance, how intimidated would you be in the presence of a platinum hit-maker?

I've read your lyrics and I agree: They do have potential.
But you're selling yourself short by fantasizing about
a relationship that is virtually unattainable. Babyface
will not fly out of the woodwork, give you a check for
a million dollars, and make you famous. But somewhere—maybe even in your class—is an artist, a writer,
or a producer who has the talent and determination to
go all the way with you. This is exactly who needs you.

Best Wishes,
Dan Kimpel

Look Around

As I mentioned in my response, as music professionals
we need to become clairvoyant, to be able to ascertain
which of those we encounter have the necessary ingredients to go all the way, and to align ourselves with them
while we have the chance. By the time someone becomes
successful, they're far too immersed in their own career
to have time to think about yours.

Music professionals are most comfortable with those
who are on the same level they are—major producers
work with major talent, and hit songwriters write for
hit artists. I have been contacted by songwriters who are
convinced that they have the next Faith Hill single. "I
just have to get it to her," they'll tell me.

There is no rule that determines that only the best
songs get recorded, only the most masterful artists get
signed to record deals, and only the most deserving
among us have long and profitable careers. Certainly
unknown songwriters also have the tools to create

stunning lyrics and music, but it's not enough to simply have these skills. Access and a reputation is necessary as well.

That's what this entire book is about. Understand, Faith Hill is a huge talent, and most of the songwriters and artists in Nashville pitch songs for her projects. So in order for unknown songwriters to even have a faint hope of getting a song to her, they first have to build a career that puts them on a par with hers. Wouldn't it make sense that an artist of this magnitude would have the finest song crafters in the music business writing songs especially for her?

Sixth Sense

Music people have finely tuned abilities to recognize and encourage future hit makers. I can recall some intriguing examples in my own history—of a young man who was living in his car on the street and two years later was sharing a mansion with Lisa Marie Presley; or the bag boy who was so friendly to all of the customers at a local supermarket and was signed with a multi-release deal for Virgin Records; or the earnest young man from Washington, D.C., whom I hired to sell $20 ads for a music trade publication who is now the president of a successful record label. This all relates to my primary creed—that we cannot make things happen, we can only put ourselves in the position for success. It take tremendous determination, force, and focus. And before this must exist belief.

Drugs in the Music Biz

When teaching a series of classes, I'll generally announce the next day's text. My declaration, "Tomorrow we'll be doing drugs and alcohol," is usually met with much applause by my young charges. Of course I don't plan to turn the hallowed halls of learning into Willie Nelson's tour bus, but in speaking to the realities of the life of a musician, certain substances bear discussion.

I'm certainly no Puritan, but regarding the myths of the musical life, it is imperative to understand what can loom in the way of success. Historically, nothing has robbed musical creators of their gifts—and their lives—like drugs and alcohol.

As a child of the '60s (actually, the '70s, but I was in Ohio, and we didn't get the '60s *until* the '70s), I observed the hijinks of the Beatles, Stones, and the various tribes of the San Francisco Bay area, all seemingly in the throes of psychedelic creation. I was stunned by the losses: Brian Jones, Jimi Hendrix, Janis Joplin, Jim Morrison. Later, the suicide of Kurt Cobain had the same impact on his fans.

Drug use affects everyone around you: Your family, your friends, your fellow musicians, and most of all, your music. For many musicians, it's a rite of passage, and not everyone moves through it intact. My judgments are based on strict professionalism only; at the level where I operate, people need to be utterly dependable. Any substance or trait that makes them less so will make others less inclined to work with them.

Most music business professionals have operated in an arena where drugs and alcohol are accepted social ingredients. I've heard it implied by certain cynics that, back in the day, record labels actually preferred a certain degree of drug dependency from artists because it made them easier to control and therefore more predictable. As always, the way a million-selling artist is perceived with or without substances will be different than the attention given to a new, or aspiring, artist. Times change; if you deduce that your career is stalled by substances, take heart. In the music cities, Narcotics and Alcoholics Anonymous meetings are terrific places to network.

On the Road with John Mayer

Reliability and consistency are trademarks of successful musicians. When I interview many rising artists, I'm aware of what they have to endure. Grammy Award winner John Mayer related these rigors to me. "To wake up at six in the morning after doing a show the night before and sing on a morning TV show, you've got to rehearse each song three times. If you're singing two songs, now you've got six songs—actually *eight* songs in the morning, including the performance. After that you go and do radio—another five songs. For every song you sing there's some jackass who didn't set the levels right. You're into the bridge and you get the international arms-waving stop sign. 'Sorry John, the level's messed up. Let me hear it from the beginning.' It turns your voice to chopped liver."

Mayer avows that constant travel, interviews, and early morning performances sap him of vocal subtlety, leaving him with only his more strident vocal tones to cut through the mix and the exhaustion. Once this whirlwind is underway, Mayer is also concerned that he's now cursing what he loves the most—singing his songs. Still, the final time in the day that he sings a song is invariably his favorite, because he shares it with a live audience. "I can play my songs a million times as long as it's in front of a crowd that wants to hear them," he proclaims, "instead of a dented microphone that some guy insists is picking up both the vocals and the guitar."

Am I Too Old to Rock?

I am not in the business of telling people what they can and cannot do. If you observe the shambling dinosaurs that make up the major-label contingent of the record business, you'll observe that young teen stars, mostly female, are signed at increasingly younger ages. Even country music—long the bastion of grizzled faces and hat-wearing journeymen—is not immune to the trends, now featuring strapping young men who wouldn't be out of place on a beefcake calendar. Much of this has to do with the rise of video as a marketing tool. Also, demographics for recorded music purchasing are younger. Let's face it, new pop music has much more influence over those in their teens than those who have moved into subsequent stages of their lives.

This is not to say that older audiences don't buy music—they do. They also buy concert tickets (and merchandise) in record numbers. But older audiences are more resistant to new music. They remain more loyal to the artists they grew up listening to.

The way we come in is often the way we are perceived, and even though we need to change career direction, others' perceptions of us keep us pigeon-holed and limited. Following is an e-mail communiqué that addresses two concerns: one of reinvention and another of ageism.

Dear Dan,

I've been a professional in the music industry for over twenty years. As many of us do, I began as a performer and a songwriter, then I developed another career, where I have worked successfully in a behind-the-scenes capacity.

Now, almost two decades later, I've decided that maybe I gave up too easily and allowed myself to be discouraged too early. In this coming year, it's my intention to return to writing songs and performing, but I'm worried about being too old. What advice would you give me?

Behind-the-Scenes Betty

Following is my reply.

Dear Betty,

As those of us know, being inside the music business is one key to success in it; in other words, in this notoriously insular industry it is virtually impossible to come from outside and make an impact. So, in this light, your two decades of experience are laudable because they have given you valuable access. However, one of the realities of having already established yourself as a behind-the-scenes functionary is that this has now become your identity.

As such, your desire to branch into another area of the business may be confusing to those around you. What would you think about a manager who confessed he actually wanted to be a songwriter, or a video stylist who was an aspiring diva? Would they be credible to you?

And yes, there is another harsh reality in our business. For more mature performers, this is a chilly climate. One need only to turn on MTV to understand that in an era of surgically enhanced nymphets, maturity is not necessarily an advantage. Unless you consider reincarnation, we are all given only one life. And many of the teen stars of today have spent that life in this business.

There are, however, many opportunities to fulfill yourself both artistically and commercially. Songwriting, for example, is an area where all that counts is the power of the song. Songwriters are not required to possess any definable type of visual allure or to be of a certain age. In fact, some of the most vibrant pop singles in recent memory have been penned by writers well into their fourth, and even fifth, decades. Synergy is power. Becoming involved in the careers of emerging artists and offering them open windows into the music business may be a viable way for you to fulfill your artistry.

If you need to write and perform to satisfy your creative soul, you should certainly do so, whether it be in a coffee house, a church, or club. But don't throw yourself into an arena with kids half your age, and don't be consumed by envy of them, either.

Your letter dictates to me that you have the creativity to carve out a viable economic niche for yourself in this business. I would recommend that you continue to apply this same creativity to expanding, reinventing, and enhancing your career while divining new outlets for your creative needs.

Good Luck,
Dan Kimpel

Critical Crises and Drama Queens

I was honored to study artist management at UCLA Extension under Ken Kragen. At the time, this venerable and well-respected manager was handling his longtime client, Kenny Rogers, who was embarking on a co-headlining tour of Canada with Dolly Parton. One night, Ken came to class having just received a call on the eve of the show informing him that the elaborate stage set that would be shared by the two artists was too large to fit into the first venue. The production manager had insisted that Ken fly north immediately to assess and rectify the situation, but Ken had no such intention. "Crises have a way of resolving themselves," he commented. Sure enough, when we convened for class the following week, Ken shared that somehow the production manager had made it work. Again, Kragen enunciated his theory that if you ignore a crisis, it will probably work itself out.

A few years later, I could hear Ken's words echoing through my head, even over the thunderous bluster of the manager of Mr. Big Producer who was inches from my face, snarling, "Look, either my client goes on stage now, or we're leaving." The occasion was the award presentation to A Hit Songwriter at an historic Hollywood theater. We had invited Mr. Big Producer to present this award, and he'd shown up with an entourage that included his fashionably hirsute and stereotypically overbearing manager. The songwriter's publicist had instructed Mr. Big Producer to arrive earlier than necessary, and his manager was adamant: Mr. Big Producer would *not* wait around. He demanded that I change the order of the show so that the award presentation would happen in the middle of the show, not at the finale.

I called the publicist on my walkie-talkie, assessed the situation for her, then disappeared into the lobby of the theater to handle another situation. Sure enough, when I poked my head backstage a half hour later, A Hit Songwriter and Mr. Big Producer were sitting and jamming on acoustic guitars, inventing an impromptu song to duet on when the award was presented. Everyone was all smiles.

This story illustrates a couple of truths. First, the manager is paid to be commanding. His only concern was his client. Often artists and producers require someone to wield absolute power. Being heavy-handed works for some managers whose agenda is the well-being of their clients. Second, when the human element was introduced to the so-called "crisis"—the music—the interaction between Mr. Big Producer and A Hit Songwriter smoothed over the situation. The music won.

Third, the publicist had erred in requesting the early arrival of Mr. Big Producer, who had left a recording session specifically to be at this event. In production, time is of the essence, and you don't want to have important people just hanging around and waiting. Fourth, as Ken Kragen taught, once all of the bluster and drama were removed from the situation, everyone was basically decent.

Ten Networking Strategies for Dispelling a Crisis

Following is a list of strategies for dealing with crises.

1. Don't be forced into making immediate decisions. Take a deep breath and remain calm.

2. Remove emotion from the equation; think logically and pragmatically.

3. Do what's right for everyone. Don't think only of covering your ass.

4. If you're not comfortable with high voltage screaming, then don't be forced into doing it. Take the opposite tact. Speak softly.

5. Be aware that some people will scream to get their way.

6. Sometimes people need to be heard. Try saying their *exact words* back to them to let them know you're listening. If someone is screaming "This stage is too small," you might reply, "I understand you think the stage is too small. But if we move the monitors off the front of the stage, reposition the drums, and slide the bass amp a little to the left, we can make it work." Make allies, not adversaries.

7. Avoid overstatements and generalizations in agitated conversation. "You never…" and "You always…" are particularly off-putting.

8. Avoid confrontational poses. Don't challenge others physically.

9. An excellent way of bridging a conflict with another person is to query, "What would you like to see happen?"

10. Remember: None of this drama will make a single iota of difference in another hundred years!

Treat Everyone with Respect

I received a breathless telephone pitch this morning from a high-powered New York publicist who requested that I interview her client, a hit songwriter of some repute, who had penned huge hits back in his day and was now resurrecting his career via a musical. Would I be interested in profiling him for an article? I hesitated not a second. "No, I wouldn't be interested," I said.

Let me tell you exactly why I rejected her proposal. When I first came to Hollywood, I was a musician and songwriter eager to gain a foothold in the music business. I had much more time than money, so I would volunteer for non-profit music organizations and work at events where I could gain knowledge and make contacts. This was not particularly glamorous work—driving across vast stretches of a then-unfamiliar Los Angeles, delivering promotional materials to music stores, lugging sound equipment, or taking telephone calls. But I did every task asked of me with enthusiasm and energy.

Later, when these organizations had budgets and a need for additional staff, they hired me.

But back to this morning's telephone call. As the publicist droned on about her client's achievements, all I could remember was years ago when he was invited to speak at an event where I was a volunteer. He showed up in a surly mood with a huge, unexpected entourage in tow. Nothing was right: The mineral water we'd provided was the wrong brand, the temperature in the hospitality room was too cold, and the food was too salty. He treated those of us who were working on the event as his personal minions, and with his every pompous demand, lorded over us with his superiority. One final note: We were in an historic meeting hall with "No Smoking" signs posted everywhere. When a member of his entourage lit up a cigarette and was subsequently asked to extinguish it, he did so by grinding the butt with the heel of his boot into the priceless mahogany floor as he chuckled with amusement.

And now, his representative is on the telephone, pleading for me to write about him, and it is my distinct pleasure to say, "No, thank you." I do not have an agenda. I don't stay up nights thinking of those who have wronged me. I think such energy is wasted and negative. However, I do play a very long game. So take this story as a word of caution, dear readers. Never step on toes connected to an ass that you may someday have to kiss.

Summary

In the music business, people don't disappear, they simply reinvent themselves and change positions. Trust me, your relationships will last much longer than any job you acquire, and you will see the same folks again and again. The way they feel about you will determine your success. I'll conclude this chapter with a quote from one of my all-time favorite interview subjects, who says it best.

"I've learned that people will forget what you said, people will forget what you did, but people will never forget how you made them feel."—Dr. Maya Angelou

CHAPTER 5

Making Contact

No other interaction has the intense dynamics of two people together in the same room. Huge corporations with every conceivable piece of technology for video conferencing and conference calls still prefer to send executives halfway around the world to close deals. The reason: Nothing has the impact of person-to-person interaction.

Body Language

The way you stand or sit makes an immediate and intuitive impression on others. I can look at a classroom full of students and instantly identify which ones are receptive to my message and any who are resistant. Open body language—standing with arms at the side and palms turned outward—reflects an attitude of receptivity. Crossed arms or, when sitting, crossed legs, indicates resistance.

When meeting others socially, your posture also projects how you feel about yourself. When you're out at a club, who do you think people notice first? The person who is standing tall and straight or the one who looks like he wants to crawl into his shell? It's amazing how something as simple as good posture can make someone look tall, slim, and most important, confident. And the confident person is the one who gets noticed for all the right reasons.

When we were children, we were told to walk with a book on top of our heads to practice good posture. But now posture starts with three activities we do every day: sitting, standing, and sleeping. Look at a mirror while standing up straight. Check out which areas are preventing you from standing up straight. Are your shoulders crouched; is your head down; is your back bent? Straighten out whatever is slouching and observe the difference. Your ears, shoulders, hips, knees, and ankles should make one straight line. Now relax your shoulders and slightly bend your knees—you don't want to look like a robot.

The major part of maintaining proper posture is reminding yourself to stand and sit straight. And this is the hardest part. Use these little tips to make sure you don't cheat:

Tell your friends. They can serve as your support system, and they will be glad to elbow you when you're caught slouching.

Use Post-It notes. Put them in areas you see daily—your medicine cabinet mirror, your rearview mirror, and your computer monitor.

Feel the results. Keep looking at the difference between a good posture and the one you see in the mirror, to really visualize the work to be done.

Exercising often, especially your back and abs, and staying disciplined will reap great physical rewards. With good posture, you'll look thinner and more confident. You'll have all the reasons in the world to stand tall and be proud.

Good Grooming

We telegraph the way we feel about ourselves to others through our physical presence. Good grooming is especially critical for anyone in the entertainment business. Poor hygiene, bad breath, or dirty clothes all transmit low-self esteem and a "who cares?" attitude.

For men, regular haircuts are recommended, but the more subtle areas need not be ignored. If your eyebrows are bushy, have your haircutter trim them or have them waxed at the local nail salon. It typically costs less than $10 and can make a marked difference in your appearance. Regular teeth cleaning is a must for good dental health, and if your teeth are stained or dull, you might want to consider the benefits of whitening them either with an over-the-counter remedy like White-Strips or better yet, a custom-made tooth tray and gel provided by your dentist. Beware the overly white, newscaster image, though (we see plenty of that in Los Angeles).

Clothes Horse

To be comfortable in any social situation, you first have to dress for the occasion. Wear clothes that fit well and are appropriate to the event. You want to feel good and comfortable in them because it's hard to mingle with confidence if you're dressed inappropriately or your clothes are ill-fitting.

Given the choice of being overdressed or under-dressed for an event, it's always preferable to be a little slicker than the occasion calls for, rather than to be perceived as a slob.

I am honored to attend the annual black-tie dinners presented by ASCAP and BMI to honor their top composers and songwriters. For the film community, black tie means old-school tuxes, white shirts, and bow ties. For the pop and R&B communities, the appropriate dress is deemed "creative black tie," which means it's OK to augment the traditional look with any number of creative options, such as ties, hats, jewelry, and so on. I've also found that a formal black suit works well instead of a tux.

Do I ever see guests dressed inappropriately at these high-end Beverly Hills functions? Yes, I once saw a well-known manager in a T-shirt., but he was accepting an award for Song of the Year on behalf of his client, so he could wear whatever he wanted. I regularly see another million-selling songwriter, female, wearing a tuxedo T-shirt. At a recent dinner, when the rock group Metallica and singer/songwriter Jackson Browne were being honored, I noted that they were dressed to reflect the pride they felt in their milestone achievements.

Music business people are tribal. Living in Hollywood, I've learned to let my instincts tell me when I'm in the presence of kindred spirits. The look is unstudied cool, a lot of black, leather, retro, and vintage clothes. Jewelry tends toward the severe with metallic chains and metal belts. Extreme hair colors come and go; facial hair styles for men—goatees, unshaven look, soul patch (the spot of hair just under the lower lip), and extended sideburns all serve the purpose of establishing cultural identity.

I always recommend wearing a conversation piece—unusual jewelry, a lapel pin, a tie, scarf, or any other distinctive object—to give others the opportunity to begin conversations with you. People are basically shy, and that strange little tchotchke on your jacket may be the key to unlocking dialogue. "What an unusual piece. Is it vintage?" might be the opening of a conversation and the beginning of a profitable relationship.

Your visual presentation is your trademark. If you're a musician, others should be able to tell what type of music you perform before you ever you play a note.

Ups and Downs in the Capitol Tower

It's an iconic piece of architecture known around the world. Looming over the intersection of Hollywood and Vine, The Capitol Tower, home to Nat King Cole, Frank Sinatra, the Beatles, and the Beach Boys, is an enduring symbol of Hollywood.

I recall interviewing Roy Lott, who was then president of the label, in a palatial conference room with a panoramic view. As engaging as Mr. Lott was, what I remember most about the interview was the ride up and down the tower in the elevator. As the elevator arrived at successive floors, I was instantly signaled what department we were in by the way the employees were dressed. Full-on suits, ties, and vests? The legal department and business affairs. Edgy, L.A. hipster attire: publicity. Edgier and more outré still? A&R. Unkempt, casually disheveled, and overly caffeinated? The musicians, of course, recording in Capitol's fabled studios. With each successive stop, the denizens were revealed to me by their attire.

Similarly, I was at a dinner party recently with a distinguished, white-haired gentleman in a black wool turtleneck. "So you're a jazz guy" I stated by way of introduction. "You can tell?" was his reply. Yes. My instincts and experience transmitted this to me, plus I subconsciously read his attitude, energy, and creativity. What this gentleman had was a distinctive "look," emblematic of jazz musicians.

What we wear as music business professionals similarly transmits information about us to others. For example, the obvious attire: T-shirts with names of bands or brands of equipment, events, or venues. When I first joined a gym in Los Angeles (a prerequisite to living here, I assure you), I would invariably work out with a music biz T-shirt on, so others in the gym would begin conversations with me. It worked. A simple piece of "swag" (free merchandise) was an invitation for others to interact.

I know of a music publisher in Los Angeles, Justin Wilde, whose company, Christmas and Holiday Music, dominates the seasonal market. I can always spot Justin at an ASCAP Membership meeting by his red and white Santa Claus hat. Not a subtle gesture. Is there any doubt what type of music he deals with? Alternative, hip-hop, and country all have their individual looks. It's tribal.

When we are introduced to another person, they make an instant, instinctive judgment of us based on factors relating only to looks. Therefore, in a music business environment, it's up to us to transmit the correct information.

Ten Visual Cues for Your "Look"

Consider the following tips for achieving the right look.

1. Identify yourself with the appropriate tchotchke: a lapel pin or something suitably subtle yet unique.

2. Extreme looks work in certain circles, but again, the goal is to attract others, not terrify them.

3. Watch out for the sex thing. I regularly attend a music business conference in a mountainous western state where nubile, aspiring young female artists congregate to attract the attention of A&R reps from L.A. and Nashville. If you're doing music, don't confuse the issue by wearing stage attire in the daytime that would be more suitable for a lady of the night. It may well telegraph a signal to the over-stimulated males of the species.

4. Casual does not mean dirty.

5. Ask your gay friends for help.

6. Watch source material, including entertainment television shows, videos, and magazine layouts in periodicals like *GQ, Details,* or *Vibe.*

7. Let your look mirror you, not limit you.

8. We are not in a conservative, drab business. Don't be too dull or conservative.

9. Make your look entertaining.

10. Learn what colors work best for you—clothes, like music, need to be in harmony.

Conversation Instigation

In researching the subjects I interview for magazine articles, videos, and in-flight audio shows, I strive to acquire a picture of the whole person, not what they project to the record buying public or to an audience full of fans.

I've learned that legendary trumpet player and founder of A&M Records, Herb Alpert, is a noted sculptor and painter. Hit songwriter/producer Glen Ballard loves to talk about Italy, especially its art and cuisine. Leonard Cohen is a Zen Buddhist, and heavyweight industry lawyer Donald Passman trains dogs.

They say in love opposites attract, but what draws us together as people are our similarities. We all come from somewhere, have families, spouses or partners, children, pets, homes. Human beings are complete packages, and their artistry and music is simply one part, which is quite often the direct result of a much larger picture. When meeting potential music industry contacts, concentrate on who they are as people, not only how you perceive them as musicians or business entities. Music people don't talk music all of the time.

Having a knack for expressing interest in others is what makes a good conversationalist. The ability to express thoughts and feelings eloquently is equally important. Including all people present is common sense, and the proportion of people who speak should be in equal division. If three people are present and one person dominates the conversation, he is not having a conversation—rather, he is giving a speech.

Ten Conversation Leaders

Being a good conversationalist requires being able to ask questions as well as excellent listening skills. Here are 10 leading questions you can ask without seeming presumptuous or nosy.

1. Are you originally from here?

2. What do you like best about living in this town?

3. Do you have many opportunities to travel?

4. Are you a film buff?

5. What's your latest favorite movie?

6. What are you listening to that I should know about?

7. Are there any great restaurants in this part of town?

8. What gym do you go to?

9. Are you a sports fan?

10. Do you have a dog or cat?

Ask questions to encourage the other person to talk, and comment on their answers to continue the conversation. Here are four types of comments you can make:

1. Expanding: "Tell me more, it sounds as if you had a great time."

2. Comparing: "That sounds as if it is similar to…"

3. Self-revealing: "I know what you mean. I was in a similar situation last year."

4. Clarifying: "What exactly did he do?"

Small talk, sure, but effective ice-breakers none the less. Note that I didn't include questions about music (I'll get to that soon enough), spouses/partners, or children. There is no reason for anyone to take offense or feel like you're prying. Conversation is like a tennis ball being volleyed back and forth across a net. Effective conversationalists know how to keep the conversation flying. Initiating it is considered a positive trait.

Asking advice is a surefire way to extend the conversation. If this doesn't work, try asking for an opinion, but remember that your proper follow-up response is not to heartily agree nor to be argumentative.

Sensitive Areas

· ·

At a music business conference in Northern California, I witnessed this uneasy interaction. One of the attendees, an Asian-American singer/songwriter, took understandable offense when a clueless music publisher quizzed her with, "So, what is your nationality?" The songwriter, of course, answered with a terse, "I'm an American."

Americans come in many shapes, creeds, and colors, so many that the tired old phrase "All-American" needs to be expunged from our modern vocabulary for good. This is not the so-denigrated "political correctness"— rather, it's correctness. "Nationality" is not "ethnicity," and besides, why would the above publisher need to know this information? Simply because the songwriter had (in the publisher's estimation) Asian features? When I was managing a recording artist from Hawaii, I recall encountering the same rudeness. "What is he?" one magazine editor said, squinting at his press photos. "A singer who writes songs and records," I answered. "No, you know what I mean. What is he?" persisted the editor.

In a listening session at a conference, I was teamed up with a major record executive from one of the most prominent record labels in the world to evaluate live talent. One of the artists, a dynamic woman of considerable power, had the room shaking with her conviction. At the conclusion of her song, the exec asked only, "So, are you married?" The singer stood in disbelief at the inappropriateness of his query.

The entertainment business is one of smoke and mirrors, and what is projected is often the image, not the entire artist. That said, we cannot afford to make assumptions about others in our business based simply on the way they appear to us. As the old saying goes, "If you 'assume,' it makes an ass out of 'u' and 'me.'"

Assumptions to Avoid About Anyone to Whom You're Introduced

Coming in contact with a variety of personalities is a trademark of our business. What you see, however, is not always what you get. Avoid making social gaffes based on assumptions regarding

- ▶ Race
- ▶ Age
- ▶ Sexual preference
- ▶ Political affiliation
- ▶ Musical likes and dislikes
- ▶ Religion
- ▶ Marital status

Complimentary Consideration

Often when I'm conducting interviews, common names will come up in conversation. During an interview with writer/producer Billy Mann, who has seen phenomenal success with artists including Jessica Simpson, Josh Groban, and many others, he referenced Pink's guitar player, my friend Rafael Moreira. "Raf is amazing," he said. As soon as the conversation was over, I called Rafael immediately to let him know that Billy had spoken so highly of him. A compliment once removed is doubly effective: It made Rafael feel good and also translated into his feelings about Billy. Meanwhile, I'll also benefit because I passed on a positive message. Speak up; if you have a nice thought, by all means share it. You can often tell more about a person by what he says about others than what others say about him.

But don't share the negative stuff or pass it on, and please, never say anything negative about any person present. This is one lesson that I almost learned the hard way. Invited by the performing rights organization of a major composer, I attended a screening of the film that he'd scored. As the end credits rolled, a ghastly song almost obliterated the mood of the picture, a song so bad, in fact, that the composer whispered to the performing rights organization's spokesperson, who subsequently announced to the room, "The composer wants you to know that he had nothing to do with choosing this song." Later that same week I was having lunch with a film agent who asked me, "Have you ever heard a piece of music in a film that was so bad you couldn't imagine why it was there?" Of course I began gleefully recounting the story of the horrific song, but fortunately, as it turned out, omitting the crucial details. "Who wrote the song?" demanded the agent. As I opened my mouth to respond I suddenly saw the songwriter I was about to malign rise up at the next table—just in time to avoid a serious faux pas on my part.

Similarly, conversation shouldn't be about someone, even in a group of close friends. If someone talks bad about another person in public, they'll probably bad mouth you as well. No matter how tempted you may be to pass along a cutting comment or to join a group talking badly about another person, don't do it. It doesn't reflect on anyone other than you, and it will make you look bad.

There are rarely regrets for what has not been said. People who speak easily often communicate too much, but someone who doesn't speak at all doesn't add to the party. In conversation, it's best to aim for the middle—know when to listen and when to carry. Many stories are best told briefly and once only. More regrets are expressed over what was said than what was not.

In ending a conversation, use exit lines because not only do you need to say hello, you need to say good-bye. An exit line will help you say good-bye gracefully and leave on a positive note. Don't strive for cleverness, just be sincere. You can simply say, "It's been nice talking to you," "Good to see you," "I hope to see you again soon," or my personal favorite, "I'm gonna go work the room." If so inclined, shake hands good-bye or place your hand lightly on the other person's shoulder to convey sincerity.

Remembering Names

When I ask a room full of participants at a seminar how many of them have problems remembering names, I'm not surprised when the majority raise their hands. One reason is that at the moment when someone we meet is saying their name, we're generally shaking their hand and our attention is diverted away from the sound. Here are three strategies for remembering names.

1. Examine a person's face discreetely when you are introduced. Locate an unusual feature—prominent ears, a precarious hairline, a projecting forehead, caterpillar-like eyebrows, etc.—and create an association between the characteristic, the face, and the name in your mind.

2. Associate the person with someone you know with the same name, or perhaps associate a rhyme or image from the name with the person's face or defining feature. The more infantile the better; you don't have to share this with anyone else.

3. Repeat the individual's name immediately after you hear it, and use it as often as possible without being obvious. If the name is unusual, ask how it is spelled or where it comes from and, if appropriate, exchange cards. The more often you hear and see the name, the more likely it is to sink in. Also, after you have left that person's company, review the name in your mind, and make notes surreptitiously in a notepad if you're really working it.

Did You Drop That Name?

I remember reading review notes from a lecture at a music school accusing me of dropping names. OK, I admit, it goes with the territory. I've programmed music heard on-board by the most powerful ruler of the free world, interviewed virtually every major recording artist in the history of American pop music, and lectured for half a decade at a college founded by an ex-Beatle. Still, the criticism hit home. I recall that the class to whom I was lecturing was not the most welcoming, and I was probably using recognizable names to prove my credibility. In retrospect, I didn't need to, since I'd written their textbook.

Many name droppers believe that if they are associated with important people, you will be impressed. They're often gravely insecure about their own achievements, so they use others' names to add to their esteem.

101

After my scathing review, I've become more sensitive about my own tendencies in this direction. (And I'll ask Clive, Alanis, Avril, Aretha, Britney, and Quincy to do the same.)

Business Cards

In this high-tech, digital world, there are few more economical ways of networking than passing out business cards. It is now possible to design and order business cards online, and in some instances you can even have cards made free. Whatever the method, your business card can communicate many things about you, and here are some tips to presenting the proper picture.

▶ Limit yourself to the business at hand. A card that reads "Joe Jones, songwriter, recording artist, dog trainer, fortune teller, high colonic therapist" lacks a positive message about your commitment to your art and will not impress the recipient.

▶ Simple is good; readability is essential. Check out business card design samples online or at your local library for tips and examples.

▶ If your career requires that you move often, consider having a blank line on which to hand write your telephone number.

▶ Keep the fonts simple, avoid the really grotesque ones, and don't crowd the information.

▶ Do include e-mail and Web site info.

▶ Refrain from crossing out numbers or addresses. Get new cards when any of your information becomes obsolete. It's a few dollars well spent.

The best time to pass out your card, obviously, is when someone asks you for it. Otherwise, offer it with an easy message. "Should you need to reach me for any reason whatsoever..." is a nice, low-key statement. Similarly, when you want someone else's card, be direct but not demanding. "What's the best way for me to reach you?" is an excellent prod.

Working the Room

Now it's time: You've been invited to a music industry event where you're sure to meet some movers and shakers. As you're about to descend into a pressure-cooker environment, it is imperative that you prepare, mentally and physically, to present yourself in the best possible light. "Working a room" is a variant of the art of mingling, of blending into any given space containing groups of socializing people and becoming part of the action. Making the transition from background to foreground, from intruder to "one of us" is no easy matter and requires considerable finesse, especially in music circles. Here are some time-tested tips.

Arrive early and spend moments of solitary time in your car relaxing and preparing yourself for the moment. If you're late you will be in danger of giving off negative, frantic energy, so having extra time to locate parking, elevators, entrances, restrooms, and escape routes is advisable.

I use this extra time to pump myself up. I might begin by affirmations, such as "I belong here" and "I'm going to be upbeat and charming." A huge part of working any room is getting fear under control.

I also review my objectives for the evening, whether it's seeing old friends or, more likely, making new contacts. Don't be afraid of talking to yourself in preparation, of articulating your intentions out loud.

I check my pockets to make sure the necessary tools are at hand. I always have an interesting and classy pen, plenty of fresh, non-dog-eared business cards in an appropriate holder, and a small notebook to jot down names or details that I may need to refer to after I leave.

Breath mints are a must. Also, if food is being served, either a toothpick or a floss stick that can be used surreptitiously in the restroom over the course of the evening is advisable. Nothing can negate a good impression like a piece of arugula sprouting through your teeth!

Give yourself time when you enter the room. It's fine to wait a while before striking up a conversation. We are sometimes so focused on ourselves that we are our own worst enemy, and often what people are most afraid of is sticking out like a sore thumb. Be easy on yourself. Learn to be alone for a while, and be comfortable. Assess the dynamics of the room and move around the perimeter. Enjoy the art, the buzz of conversation. Take away the pressure by imagining that no one can see you.

Another advantage of early arrival is having an opportunity to meet the host or hostess and to enjoy the food before the buffet gets mobbed and before you need to expend your energies on communicating rather than scarfing the free crab cakes.

Be very aware of your reaction to alcohol. For some, a drink or two can be very helpful in assuaging anxiety, but nothing can be more detrimental to creating a good impression than being under the influence of demon liquor. A wine spritzer—wine diluted with soda water—may be a good compromise. Pace yourself.

Prepare to move on. Finding someone—anyone—to talk to is the only goal of most crowd-phobic people. You will be perceived as needy if you cling to the first person who says hello.

A great method in working a room is to seek out people who are standing alone. Introduce yourself, find out why they are attending the event, and then offer to introduce them to someone they might want to meet. Remember, if you walk into a room and you're only there to take, people will pick up on that. But if you're a person who gives, it's easy for others to give to you in return.

Follow the 10-5 rule for meeting and greeting: If you make eye contact with someone within 10 feet of you, you must acknowledge them with a nod or a smile. At five feet, you should say something—"Hello" or "Good evening." Don't pretend you don't see them.

I learned this next lesson the hard way. If five people are in conversation, feel free to join them; four people, sure, walk right up; three, no problem. But beware: If two people are engrossed in conversation, unless you know them very well, it is *never* permissible to intrude. Odds are, they're discussing something private (maybe even you!).

Have you ever been in conversation with someone who seems to find whatever is over your shoulder more interesting than you? Being a good listener is the most important part of being a great conversationalist. Don't let your eyes wander. If the person you're speaking to does this, follow his stare with a wry comment, "I wanted to see what was so fascinating."

Hidden Opportunities

One of the famous disadvantages of living in the hills of Los Angeles is that they sometimes tumble down. Such was the case this winter, as a mountain of mud surged through my street on its inevitable, gravity-determined path. As I walked through the neighborhood surveying the damage, I came upon my neighbor, who was speaking with a couple who had recently relocated to the block. As I was introduced to them, the male member of the pair commented, "Jean [my neighbor] tells me I can hear you on United Airlines." When I asserted that, yes, I did frequently voice shows for the in-flight entertainment, he told me, "I'm in animation, and we always need voices. Get me a CD and I'll see what I can do." How cool is that? From a mountain of mud shone a window of opportunity.

I was reminded of a singer/songwriter friend of mine, Beth Thornley, whose songs can be heard on the new DVD releases of *Dawson's Creek: Season 2* and *Roswell* and on episodes of *The Chris Isaak Show, The New Ride with Josh and Emily,* the CBS film *It Must Be Love,* and *Book of Ruth.* She tells of a serendipitous day when UPS delivered a color printer to her door that she hadn't ordered. "I called UPS and said, 'This isn't mine,'" she remembers. "'Could you come back, pick it up, and deliver it to the person whose address is just around the corner and down the street?'" "They said, 'If we do, we'll charge you for shipping.' I said, 'OK, I'll just take it.'" She called the rightful recipient, who came over to claim it, and he happened to be a music supervisor. "That was my *Roswell* placement," says Thornley, "but it was a full year down the road."

After that, Thornley recalls that she would often encounter him walking his dog, and he'd tell her what he was working on. "Also, I did a version of 'Eleanor Rigby' for another show that got canceled before they used it. I burned it to CD and asked him if I could drop it in his mailbox." Thus began a tactic by which Thornley stayed in supervisors' minds. "When I get done with something nice, I'll burn a CD and drop it into the mail for them. That keeps me in their thoughts between albums. I'm working on my second album now, but I can get one thing down and send it out as a taste. This music supervisor gave me that idea. I was close enough to hand it to him, but I thought, 'Why not send it to everyone I know?'"

Granted, Thornley and I live in an entertainment capital, but the point is that many things in our music world happen as the result of simple, chance human interactions. But you have to be ready to receive and recycle the energy. If I was walking down my street angry and muttering at the watery fate that had mired my car, or if Beth Thornley felt put-upon by her chore, the same opportunities would not have happened.

Any place can become an arena for meeting others. Neutral environments—airports, waiting rooms, and so on—are perfect places to practice "Pop People Power." You have nothing to lose and everything to gain. Let your instincts guide you, invent a reason to begin a conversation, and see where it may lead you. You could be surprised.

I often play a game when I'm waiting to catch flights, especially to or from Los Angeles, London, New York, or Nashville. I will spot the most interesting person in the waiting area and focus my attention on them. Then, if and when the time is right, I will initiate a conversation. It's a fascinating way to pass the time, and I've made innumerable contacts in my professional and personal life in airports.

Practice Makes Perfect

Just as musicians study and practice musical instruments, you also have to rehearse your networking chops and practice being open to others. You may be projecting your accessibility when you become aware if it. The following communication came to me shortly after I conducted a networking seminar as part of an educational series at a local music store.

Dear Dan,

I attended your presentation at West LA Music in the valley about a week and a half ago. I spoke with you briefly afterwards about being from Ohio. You might enjoy some feedback about your presentation.

One of the things you said that really stuck with me was the idea of practicing the networking chops. The example you used was talking to people on elevators. So, I have been doing that since that night, just to practice breaking the ice.

But here's the cool thing that has been happening to me since I started: About half of the time, before I even initiate the conversation, the other person starts talking to me. That has never happened before in my life, and now it's happened about five times in the last two weeks. The only thing I can figure is that my willingness to speak to the other person projects as openness, a quality that I didn't used to express. I'm starting to get a sense of how the process of networking really snowballs.

Thanks again for taking the time out of your schedule to share your experiences that night. I'm excited about this new unexplored skill I'm starting to develop!

Michael B.

It's true, that your openness and willingness to communicate to others can be felt, and you just never know. I'll sometimes reflect backwards, "If I hadn't gone to that party, been introduced to that person, had that conversation, and made that follow-up call, this opportunity would have never existed."

So get yourself out there; nothing happens if you don't.

The Fine Art of the Studio Hang

Is there any place more intriguing than a recording studio? Having come up in the mega-tracking rooms of Nashville and New York, it was somewhat disconcerting to move to Los Angeles and find myself in recording sessions taking place in renovated garages in the far reaches of the San Fernando Valley.

This was only a precursor of what was to come. Today, studios can be anywhere—in a home, a basement, an unused bedroom, or even a bus. Hanging out in the studio, however, is still a time-honored tradition and requires a strict adherence to protocol. Following are some tips for proper studio etiquette.

1. Never give your opinion unless you're asked. There is a strict hierarchy in the studio. The producer is in charge but in service to the artist. If you are there as a guest, it is in everyone's best interests, especially yours, that you not disturb the chemistry. The producer knows exactly what he or she is listening for in a take. Often it's emotion versus technical perfection.

2. Stay visually engaged with those recording when they come in for playback. Don't read, check your e-mail, or act bored. Again, the chemistry in a session situation is supercharged and, depending on the artist, can be very volatile. Distractions or negativity can alter the fragile emotional parameters.

3. Pay attention to everything during tracking—be very present. Look at the session as a learning experience and take in everything. What changes is the engineer making? How are the mics placed? What is the producer going for in the session?

4. Don't set anything on the recording board or any other equipment—ever. This should be self-explanatory, but a drink spilled into a console could render a priceless piece of gear inoperable. At the Liverpool Institute

for Performing Arts (LIPA) where I've lectured, they maintain a hard and fast rule that no beverages of any kind are permitted in the studio. The only exception I observed was the popping of a champagne bottle to christen "The Sir George Martin Studio." The fact that Sir George himself was sipping the bubbly made it OK.

4. If conflicts arise, make yourself invisible. Making yourself invisible also comes in handy so you don't distract any of the recording personnel. Don't announce your arrival and departure; rather, slip into the room and ascertain the vibe first. If you have to slip out, do so unnoticed.

5. Don't distract the talent with needless chatter. Vocalists are notoriously temperamental. Loading them up with your opinions, ideas, or suggestions could blow their concentration. Non-verbal communication may be your strongest option. Again, be very positive and supportive, if only through eye contact and a smile.

CHAPTER 6

Telephone and E-Mail

Cell phones, computers, BlackBerries (portable digital devices that can send and receive digital and telephone communications), and whatever might be developed by the time you've finished reading this chapter are all mechanisms that should be integrated into your networking strategy of communication.

Different methods of communication work for different individuals, and timing of your communication can be as crucial as access. Below is a common scenario that happens when you try to communicate with busy people.

Dear Dan,

I recently met a major music industry player who was kind enough to give me his card. I've been calling his office ever since then, and I haven't been able to get a hold of him. His receptionist keeps saying he's either not there or is "in a meeting." What can I do to get through to him? Should I keep on calling?

Puzzled in Pacomia

OK, this is easy: No, don't keep calling; change media. If calls don't work try, e-mail; if e-mail doesn't work, send a fax; if a fax doesn't work, send a card or letter.

It's difficult to understand the realities and demands of those with whom we communicate. Speaking from my own experience, when I'm on a writing deadline, a telephone call from someone who is not communicating about the matters at hand is usually an unwanted intrusion. At these times an e-mail is preferable because it's something I can respond to on my own terms and time.

Sometimes the opposite is true—I'm tired of writing, don't want to read e-mail, would love to stand up from the computer, and could use a distraction. At these moments I welcome calls.

But when something isn't working for you, don't continue to try to bludgeon your contacts. Simply try another avenue.

The Telephone

Next to human contact, the telephone is probably the most intimate method of communication. Think about it: You're right in someone's ear when you're speaking. The sound you project on the phone is just one element of your communication. Like all other networking strategies, effective telephone communication is determined by the ability to read the emotions and thoughts of the person on the other end of the line, not simply talking at them.

In my first year in Los Angeles, as I struggled to gain a foothold in the music business and needed to find other ways to pay the rent, telephone work—surveys, sales, soliciting—was a time honored method of making money for musicians and struggling actors. Whereas most of my co-workers resented these jobs, I found them fascinating because I learned so much about human nature by way of the intimate communication. Many of the skills I developed and use to this day were honed by making thousands of calls to people who initially had no desire to speak to me. It was wonderful training for the future, and I've never hesitated to make an outgoing call since.

Sound

The actual sound you make on the telephone should be well modulated and pleasing to the ear. Take cues from the person with whom you're speaking. Research indicates that if you talk just a little faster than the person with whom you're conversing, you'll be considered more intelligent. Certainly this is a challenge if you're talking to someone in New York City, but try listening to, and then matching, the rhythms of the person on the other end of the line.

Eating, drinking, lip smacking, or being too close to the phone are all negative signals.

Reflections of Power

The true power brokers who use the telephone use a time-honored trick: They have mirrors within close proximity, positioned so that they can see themselves speaking, to remind themselves to smile on the telephone. Try it: A smile can actually be heard. Also, to project energy and forcefulness into a telephone conversation, stand up when you make the call.

The best times to make calls in the music business are Tuesdays, Wednesdays, and Thursdays, preferably before lunch. It's most effective to make groups of calls all at once, to psyche yourself into a frame of mind where all you're doing is making calls and not diluting your energy by breaking up the flow.

Make business calls during business hours. If I receive a call at my office on weekends (yes, I'm often here but don't always answer), it telegraphs to me that the person making the call is a "part-timer" and certainly not a music business professional. Similarly, if I'm considering working with a prospective client and they call me at night, on weekends, or on holidays, it makes me not want to become involved because it tells me that they won't respect my privacy or my time.

Begin by telling your callee the purpose of the contact. "Let me tell you why I'm calling," is always helpful. "Here's the situation," is another effective intro. "I'll be brief," prepares your contact with the knowledge that it's not going to be a lengthy encounter. You need to script your call—not word for word, but outline any main points you need to include. Then get right to the point. "I have four things to discuss with you," will show the recipient of your call that you're organized and ready to do business. "How are ya?" is a cliché and should never precede a conversation with someone you don't know well.

A time-honored basic business rule is this: If you make the call, it's your responsibility to end the call because the person who makes the call is always in the driver's seat. Many heavy-duty executives make only outgoing calls.

Telephone Basics

People are enthralled by the sound of their own names. You'll need to address the person you're speaking to by name approximately once per minute to hold their attention. Don't talk at people, and listen not only to words, but to the emotions behind them. If the person you've contacted sounds harried, harassed, or as if on a deadline, be sensitive to this, and ask for a future telephone appointment with something like, "When would be a good time for us to speak?"

"I'm just calling to touch base with you" is a statement that never fails to elicit a response from me, and not a good one. It tells me that the caller has no real information to impart, that they're probably trolling me for information, and that they're playing some arcane game where, for no apparent reason, I have been designated the base. Never call someone without something specific to say. Let them know clearly the purpose of the communication, and not simply some vague notion of "It's been a long time since we spoke." Maybe there's a reason for that. If you're calling to "touch base" with me, then we are playing a game. But I make the rules—and you're out.

If you're receiving an incoming call of importance, move away from your computer so you won't be tempted to check your e-mail while you're on the phone. Yes, I know, it's a multi-tasking world, but transmitting the tell-tale clicking of a computer while you are supposedly concentrating on a telephone conversation will project insincerity. Also, kill the background music, relegate rambunctious children to another area, and dismiss yipping dogs from the room when making outgoing calls.

Music biz execs have key staff members to deflect calls, and you'll generally encounter a gate-keeper. This is an opportunity for outreach. Introduce and ingratiate yourself to key staff, because often your access to the boss will be determined by your persuasive techniques with these subordinates. Don't try to con or bully them; it won't work. Tell a short version of your story; explain briefly exactly why you're calling. When I had a receptionist working for me, she would often intervene on behalf of a caller who had made repeated attempts to get through, and I always heeded her advice.

Telephone Tracking

Having lists of people to call has proven to be very effective for some savvy networking folks: an "A" list of contacts to be spoken to weekly, a "B" list of bi-weekly contacts, and a "C" list of associates to be contacted on a monthly basis. Although you can invent reasons to call people, this invariably works best if it has some basis in fact. "I saw an article that made me think of you," is an effective ice-breaker.

It's helpful to take notes on conversations to avoid repeating yourself and to recall details of specific interactions. Mega Hollywood execs often have an assistant listening in on the line to do just this.

Cell Phones: Antennas of Satan?

Has there ever been a device invented that is so convenient yet so utterly abused as the ubiquitous cell phone? I won't add to the chatter on this matter other than to say that I've had a cell phone for many years, and that I was possibly as irritating when I first got it as many of the folks I currently witness. Of course, back then it was a novelty. Today, everyone from children to drug dealers are plugged in and chattering away, usually cluelessly. Not only is using a cell phone no longer impressive in any way (unless it's some incredibly new modern one), but when it is used for that reason, the user can be immediately identified as a neophyte and a poseur. A new term, "absent/present," has been coined to identify compulsive cell phone users and the phenomenon wherein an individual is there physically, but far away in conversation. It invariably throws off our sense of communication since we are isolated from those wired into their phones.

People with whom I work may call me whenever and however they wish. But when my first telephone contact with someone who calls me is via cell phone, it sets off a red flag. For instance, if I receive a call from an unknown party who uses a cell phone between the hours

of 12:00 P.M. and 2:00 P.M., I assume that they're working a "straight" job and are using their lunch hour to
make personal—or in this case, allegedly professional—
calls. This thought process invariably distracts me, and I
can't take them seriously. Not a good first impression to
give.

If someone I know in passing calls me from their cell
phone, I surmise that they're in circumstances where
they need to kill time and are using me to do so. Again,
not good. Am I an afterthought? Did a tiny piece of pro-
toplasm with the image of my face on it float through
someone's consciousness?

I sometimes receive calls where the first thing I hear
is the roaring of traffic. Has the 101 freeway called me? If
I'm getting a call from the driver of a car, it's an immediate turn-off and tells me it's someone who has chosen
to jeopardize others' lives for the sake of their own con-
venience. (In England and Japan, talking on the phone
while driving is a punishable offense. Not so in L.A.)

Cell phones are not even telephones—they're radios,
and they sound crummy. To a sonically oriented person
such as myself, it's irritating, and as such, calls are lost
and dropped. Nothing infuriates me so much as when
someone calls me on a nasty, buzzy cell phone, bellows
into it, and then drops the call. I generally don't answer
when they call back and instead let my voicemail pick
up. Also, unless absolutely imperative, I won't make outgoing calls to numbers that I recognize as cell phones
unless absolutely necessary.

If you're forced by circumstances to make an outgoing call and you have no option other than to use your

cell phone, please excuse yourself immediately when the callee answers. "I'm so sorry to have to call you on the cell, but you asked me to contact you at noon, and this was the only way." Then proceed with the call, hopefully making it brief. Brevity is the key. Elongated conversations on the cell are a strain. I can tell if someone is calling me from a cell because of the artificial way they are talking—the dreaded "cell yell." If your signal is weak, speaking louder won't help, unless of course the person is actually within earshot.

However, used effectively, the cell phone can be a marvelous device. I was representing a band and attempting, quite unsuccessfully, to book them into a local hot spot. I'd sent the press kit and CD, of course, but had been unable to contact the booker in person to do the all-important follow-up, so I decided to take more immediate action.

One afternoon, I parked in the venue's parking lot and, using my cell phone, made a call to the club and asked for the booker. When I received the "He's not available," rebuff, I determined that he was actually there. I'd dressed for the occasion in music biz garb: a nice sport jacket over an industry T-shirt, well-buffed shoes, and I carried a briefcase. I presented myself to the receptionist and announced that I was there for a meeting with the booker. Sure enough, he quizzically ventured out to greet me, invited me back to the office, and we sat down for business. He ended up booking the band, and it was the beginning of a lucrative, long-term relationship with a very happening club.

In retrospect, I think the booker might have imagined that we'd arranged this meeting and that he'd forgotten it. When using these types of tactics to get in front of the individuals you need to get to, it's important that your motives and mechanisms remain transparent. If I'd begun our meeting by guffawing, "Hah, I fooled you!" it's doubtful that I would have been able to book the band. Indeed, I may have gotten booted out the door.

But selling is selling, whether it's music or cars, and getting to the buyer is the fundamental first step. In this case, the cell phone confirmed the booker's presence for me.

Cell Phone Etiquette

To avoid unfortunate confrontations with others, you might want to observe a few basic rules of cell phone etiquette.

- ▶ Think of your phone as a portable answering machine. When you're in an appropriate place—a parked car, outside of a restaurant, etc.—you can return calls.
- ▶ If you simply must be available for a caller, put your phone on "vibrate" mode if you're in any non-private place.
- ▶ Practice speaking in a quiet conversational tone. If no one looks your way while you're speaking on your cell phone, you've got it. This is the only acceptable tone of voice.
- ▶ If you forget both "off" and "vibrate," and your phone rings in any non-private place, turn it off instantly (and as unobtrusively as possible so nobody will suspect you are the jerk responsible). No matter what: Don't answer.

Do you really want to be available all the time? Does that truly make you more productive, or does it just spread your productivity thinner over more time? A cell phone is a wonderful tool, but it's also a leash. Cell phone conversations interfere with the person-to-person contact that you might otherwise enjoy. The random conversation you might have with a person while waiting in a line, a stranger you might encounter and interact with, is instead being supplanted by the impersonal 24/7 access everyone has to you.

E-Mail

What did we do before e-mail? I find that in my world, my phone calls have probably dropped in volume by half in the past couple of years, while e-mails have increased dramatically. E-mail will never take the place of the telephone or an in-person contact, but it's a terrific way to keep in touch with both business and personal contacts. By checking my e-mail at an Internet café in Istanbul, I was once able to secure a valuable writing gig that required me to make an immediate response.

E-mail cannot, however, transmit much emotion or energy. Also, humor may fall flat, and sarcasm is almost impossible to convey. Here are some brief guidelines for composing your e-mail messages.

▶ Check that you're sending e-mail to the correct destination. Horror stories abound about those who have inadvertently sent e-mail communications to their bosses, enemies, etc.
▶ Watch out for "funny" jokes or cute stories. You might send these to your friends or family, but

they have no place in business. Ditto for warnings about "scams" or messages about a virus that is supposed to devour everyone's hard drives or the United States government's dismantling of National Public Radio. Check www.snopes.com for Urban Folk Tales first.

► Avoid attachments if you can—better to cut and paste in the body of an e-mail than to include something that your recipient may not be able to open.

► Messages should be concise and to the point. Think of it as a telephone conversation, except that you are typing instead of speaking. Keep in mind that some people receive hundreds of e-mail messages per day.

► If something is important, it should be reflected in your text, not in your punctuation. Don't use !!!!! or ALL CAPS.

► In the quest to save keystrokes, users have traded clarity for confusion: "FYI" and "BTW" are OK, but don't overuse acronyms—write out everything else.

► Use :-) and similar symbols (a.k.a. "emoticons") sparingly, if at all.

► In casual introductions, you can probably bypass the standard formalities, and just use something like "Dear Edward," or just "Edward." In the business realm, things are much more complicated, so each situation will need to be evaluated on its own. If you normally address a person as Miss/Mrs./Ms./Mr., then address them identically in e-mail.

► If your e-mail address is a business address, include your title and company name in the signature, because in the e-mail world letterheads are not used. Always include your telephone number somewhere in your e-mail.

E-mail is a conversation that does not require an immediate response. If a hundred people send you e-mail in one day, so what? You won't have to talk to them, so just think of all the hellos, good-byes, and other unnecessary chit-chat you've avoided. With e-mail you deal only with essentials, and you deal with them on your own time. That's the blessing; the curse is that it's impersonal and cold, and cannot transmit energy, enthusiasm, or warmth. Like any other networking tool, e-mail is simply one component of a much larger picture. It will never supplant the power of one-on-one communication, but it can support it.

CHAPTER 7

Creating Effective Tools of the Trade

Coming up through the ranks of popular music, we are often so intent on putting ourselves out there, trying to make ourselves known and recognizable, that we leave little air in the room for breathing. I learned long ago that the most powerful position to come from is not when you're pitching, but when someone requests something from you.

We have much more control over this than we might imagine. When I was managing artists, I ascertained that I would encounter immediate resistance if I tried to push the artists into people's faces with a heavy-handed agenda. Often the opposite tack—a soft sell—worked far better. Describing the artists I was handling in non-off-putting terms or showing a press photo or a logo or wearing a merchandise T-shirt with the artists' image, I would be questioned, "Who is that?" When I would explain (with a short pre-engineered "sound bite"), I would invariably be asked, "May I get a press kit and CD? I'd love to hear what you're up to."

Press Kits

Like most music biz professionals, I get a sixth sense about artists from their presentation; sometimes, in fact, I can tell the quality of the music even before I open the envelope containing their press kit. How? First I look at the envelope it comes in. Is it finger-printed, dirty, or dog-eared? Odds are, the music is equally a shambles. Has it been addressed to "Dear Journalist?" Not a good sign. And since the magazines I write for change location often, has the sender checked the address before mailing, or is it arriving with a forwarding mail notice on the front?

All of these are signs I look for before I open the package. Once I do begin to open it, I note the ease in doing so. Will I need a machete to tear through the layers of tape holding the envelope closed? As I pull out a package, I inevitably recall the enterprising recording artists who packaged a press kit with handfuls of glitter that subsequently embedded themselves in the plush carpeting of my office. I discovered remnants of their presentation for months after, and it always reminded me of them, but not with love.

You need to tailor-make your press kit according to whom you're sending it. I've heard managers and record company A&R personnel swear up and down that a fancy press kit isn't necessary. As a journalist, I appreciate a well-written bio, succinct press clippings, and a professional photo—either color or black and white—suitable for scanning and inserting in a magazine. It's a nice touch to have downloadable, high-resolution photos on your Web site as well.

Keep your presentation envelope size standard. An interesting, eye-catching color is permissible if the music is equally colorful. Also, use standard first-class mail. Nothing predisposes me to *not* like a band more than waiting in an interminable post office line to pick up a mystery package that requires my signature. Keep in mind that most post office box addresses do not accept UPS or FedEx, so check before mailing.

The Folder

At any given moment, I have an identical stack of black glossy folders sitting on my desk. Do you know what's in them? Well, neither do I, since there is nothing on the cover in the way of identification. Without a logo, a sticker, or something on the front of your folder, the recipient has nary a clue as to what it contains. The folder doesn't have to be extravagant, although color-coordinating it with other materials in your press kit will display a sense of unity. And unity is the most important concept to grasp when putting together a press kit. All of the visual elements have to reinforce and reflect the music because odds are it will be heard as the recipient is reading the enclosed materials.

The Cover Letter

For cover letters, short, sweet, and to the point is the best advice. Professional-looking letterhead and good-quality paper will help you achieve a positive impression. Tell the reader who you are and especially why you're sending the enclosed materials. If you're sending to a journalist, let her know that you're hopeful of a review. If you're sending to a club booker, your materials should include information pursuant to your live show. A generic letter addressed to "Dear Sir/Madam" is not sufficient. Spell out the name of the person you're addressing and be sure to render their title correctly.

Be sure to include all of your contact information on every piece of material you submit: name, address, telephone number, e-mail, and Web site.

A CD or DVD

If you have a fully produced CD, it will no doubt be included in your presentation kit, of course. Depending on to whom you're submitting, you may want to limit your exposure. For A&R at record labels or a music publisher, for example, three songs should be sufficient. If the listener wants to hear more, he can always request additional material from you, which is a good position for any fledgling band or artist to be in.

A video presentation is great for certain artists but a dicey proposition for others because a tacky, sub-par performance video can diminish the viewer's opinion of the band or artist substantially. However, I've seen impressionistic, arty videos that mirror the music, and these can be effective. Just like the CD, it may not be necessary to deluge your contacts with too much information. If you have a video, you may want to reserve it as support material for further down the line.

The Bio

I have probably written over 300 artist bios in my career. Many times harried journalists have cut corners by appropriating the exact words I've written in a bio into an article. This is totally acceptable, of course; I create bios as works-for-hire for a fee, and I don't maintain control over them once they leave my computer.

I maintain that a bio is the cement that holds a press kit together. Your bio should

► Create an identity.
► Define a musical style.
► Lead the reader directly to the music.

Recording artists, songwriters, performers, and producers all benefit from well-written bios. "Send your music, bio, and picture" is usually the first request from someone interested in your talents. If you don't have major credits, your bio can spotlight personalities, histories, and creative processes. The bio must be honest, but the truth should also sound as good as possible. Never mistake hype for substance. Such key phrases as "eagerly anticipated" and "critically acclaimed" always set off my B.S. meter. Beware the hackneyed cliché, the imprecise metaphor, the goofy, strained adjective. "Unique" means nothing to me. "Joe Jones is a brilliant artist" doesn't show, it tells. "Sue Smith is destined for stardom" is lame and off-putting. The bio must lead the reader to his own conclusions. Telling a reader what to feel or think may lead to the exact opposite impression. Double check for proper punctuation, grammar, and spelling.

Stating the style of music the artist creates in a bio is a necessity. "We don't like being pigeon-holed" is a complaint I hear often from young bands and artists. Guess what? There is a reason that retail CD stores have categories for music; otherwise buyers would never know where to look.

A bio is not a résumé, where specific information is required and a certain format is followed. There are no hard and fast rules, though there are things to be avoided. Your bio is what the stranger who is listening to your demo for the first time is holding in his or her hand. Make it reflective of who you are as an artist. Be creative. A well-written bio can make the listener want to hear your music. It can even affect the way someone listens, causing them to listen a little more closely or to be more inclined to give you the benefit of the doubt.

One of my pet peeves is reading an artist's bio that includes something along these lines: "Susie Stiletto combines the sensitivity of Joni Mitchell fused to the aggressive lyricism of Alanis Morissette, combined with the melodicism of Sheryl Crow." I know how I feel about these artists, but dropping their names in as a comparison doesn't really tell me anything about "Susie Stiletto." She'd certainly need to be a mind-blowing, powerhouse artist to rank comparison to this triumvirate.

Do not include facts that don't have to do with the music. For instance, it may be pertinent to say you ride horses if you have songs about horses or have written songs while riding horses or can draw some correlation between horses and music. Otherwise, leave those horses in the pasture. Information about your educational background, work experience, broken marriage, prison term, or dysfunctional childhood should be referenced only as it relates to the music.

If you're an artist, you probably know how difficult it is to be objective about your music and career. You'd be well advised to ask a local journalist to write your bio for you. The length is usually one page. If you've got a fascinating history and it's extremely well written, a one and a half to two-page bio is permissible. $150–$350 is the standard rate in Los Angeles. Be involved in the writing process—you can ask for drafts and rewrites.

As a journalist, I receive an average of 15 to 20 major or indie label press kits weekly. There is no singular bio style that is appropriate for all of these artists. A seething, pierced, neo-punk aggregation and a soothing, cerebral new-age artist can't possibly share the same metaphors. Your bio must speak in the same voice as your music.

Following is an example bio.

Luis Villegas — Bio

Each of Luis Villegas' label releases has revealed the unfolding artistry of a master guitarist and composer. Now, *Casa Villegas* (Baja/TSR) marks his debut as a producer. "I had a dual life, not only writing and arranging the songs, but figuring out what instruments to use, setting up the sessions, and booking the studio," says Villegas. He had the bases covered until the night before his initial session. "I'd forgotten to book the musicians," he laughs.

It's clear that Villegas and his tight-knit community of world-class players were ready for the challenge that began this two-month recording process. With Villegas' blistering nylon-string guitar at the forefront, *Casa Villegas* marks a breathtaking musical odyssey from the gritty streets of the city to the sunswept plazas of Spain, across the plains of Morocco to the ancient temples of India. Middle Eastern percussion and Indian tabla provide an aural backdrop as African bata drums mesh with congas and timbales in a wealth of musical cultures.

The rhythms of East Los Angeles, Villegas' birthplace, fuel the opening song, "Bienvendos," (Welcome) and the Latin/jazz grooves of "Whittier Blvd." Two songs featuring vocals by lyricist/vocalist José Garcia balance the instrumental mix—"Ojos Verdes" was inspired by Luis's daughter, Krista, while "Mujer Enamorada" is dedicated to his wife, Gloria. "She's in love with life and living," Luis says, "I told José, 'Write some lyrics that go with that,' and he hit the nail on the head."

Each song on the album is framed as a distinctive vignette. "I didn't want to be limited to my live instrumentation," explains Luis, who used violin, a horn section, keyboards, and additional guest vocalists. Sonic minimalism is illustrated in the austere simplicity of "Recuerdos de Jerz" featuring flamenco singer Maria Benjumeda, and "Jaleo," a song with only two guitars and percussion. Both recall a golden period Villegas spent in Spain. "It's a feeling that you're standing right in front of the street musicians on the banks of the Guadalquivir River."

Villegas channels a rhythmic physicality into "From the Heart," and a gentle samba groove informs "Brazilian Magic." Inspired by the transcendent textures of Indian music, "Kama Sutra" conjures up a frenetic mystic whirlwind of Villegas' guitar and Charlie Bishart's violin.

New audiences were introduced to Villegas via his previous album, *Spanish Kiss* (Baja/TSR) as the single "La Reyna" landed on Smooth Jazz play lists coast to coast. Corresponding appearances at high profile festivals, including the Catalina JazzTrax Festival, The Playboy Jazz Festival, and The Sedona Hot Latin Jazz Festival, sealed his reputation as a blistering live performer, while tracks from his debut CD, *Café Olé* (Domo), landed in Warner Bros., HBO, Sundance, and Warren Miller films. On record, he can be heard on *Guitar Greats* Volumes I and II (Baja/TSR); *Music for the Spirit*, Volumes I, II, and III (Domo); *Tabu Mondo Flamenco* (Narada); the *Lost & Found* soundtrack (Capitol); and *Gypsy Magic* (EMI/Virgin).

As his ever-growing body of work reflects his musical maturation as a guitarist, composer, and producer, his themes mirror his real life as a husband and father. Although this time out his creative geography is charted with a global compass, the music always comes home to *Casa Villegas*.

Your Photo

Photos for newspapers and magazines can be transmitted electronically, For most uses, low-resolution shots are fine, but for magazines you'll need a high-resolution photo. Having more than one shot is ideal, and a live picture of a band can generate more energy and vibe. Also, having a selection of black-and-white and color shots for specific uses is an excellent calling card. For your press kit, however, limit yourself to one defining shot. Don't pose in front of branches and trees that appear to grow out of your head, and make sure the shot conveys the exact attitude of your music.

Full-Court Press

There are many types of media, and each one is very specific regarding its needs. Before contacting any member of the press, you need to have a focused strategy.

Are you currently performing? If so, press releases and calendar notices to print media should be sent well in advance. Monthly publications will need pertinent information up to two months in advance of the publication date, weekly publications need at least two weeks, and dailies need at least a week in advance.

Many major publicists prefer to work press concurrent with a tour. If you're doing it for yourself, compile press lists and contacts for each city you're visiting, contact the press well in advance, and always follow up.

Do you have a story? The press always prefer an "angle," but it can't be something artificial, corny, or contrived.

National press is extremely hard to come by and won't do you any good if the reader can't immediately go to a familiar Web site or a retail outlet and pick up a copy of your CD.

Press is cumulative: The more you get, the more the press will be interested in what you've got to offer.

Include a cover letter and state exactly why you're sending information. Make sure that the person to whom you're sending your info is still at the publication and is the proper recipient for your info. Don't assume they'll pass your materials on down the line, and do not address your cover letter to "Dear Journalist." As a feature journalist and columnist for a magazine, I am not predisposed to assist anyone who hasn't bothered to do their homework and sends me materials for which I have no use. A profile, a review, a calendar listing—all are completely different functions of a magazine or newspaper. Learn who does what and address them correctly. An e-mail query to an editor is a good method.

Journalists are usually slammed with deadlines and subsequently are quite disorganized. Major record labels will often send me duplicate materials, once by e-mail and once by snail mail. Having high-resolution photos on your Web site could make the difference in you being covered, since journalistic decisions are often made at the last possible second and because something else has fallen out. The creation of magazine columns is much less objective than it may appear, and the decision to use your photo may be made by a photo or art director who doesn't care what you sound like, but only what you look like.

Begin with local press and move up accordingly. It's not necessary—in fact, it's even considered unprofessional—to thank the press unduly for doing their job. A simple "Thanks, you nailed it," note is always appreciated. Unless there is an embarrassing and glaring error in the piece that requires a retraction, don't correct them by calling attention to some insignificant detail that might be incorrect.

Follow up accordingly, but don't harass the press. Yes, in rare cases you can wear them down, but keep your desperation at bay.

Personal contacts and recommendations are still your strongest suit. In my world, a multiplicity of images makes the strongest impact. I'll read a press item, hear a song on National Public Radio, and have a friend tell me about a new act, often all in the same day.

Credibility in the Credits

I have honed a method to streamline my listening process for the volume of packages I receive weekly. First, I put aside the obvious clunkers (e.g., polka bands interpreting the music of The Police, *20 of Your Favorite Patriotic Songs*, etc.). Next, I select the releases from those artists I love (generally a small pile, I assure you). Then I look for artists and songwriters who will be of the most interest to the publications and assorted electronic media outlets for whom I provide content. After I've sifted through the major label offerings, I'm left with independent releases of which I have no prior knowledge.

While I listen to the music, I read the one-sheet (a slick sheet prepared especially for retail) and bio and scan the liner notes and the inside CD cover looking for the names of people I recognize who are involved with the project. Though seeing these names may make me want to listen, sometimes names give me other information.

To illustrate, I've invented an imaginary artist, Harry Haze, whose package I've just opened. Here's what he tells me on his album:

All Songs written by Harry Haze
Produced by Harry Haze
Published by Harry Haze Music
All Songs performed by Harry Haze
Guitar, bass, drums, keyboards by Harry Haze
Cover art by Harry Haze
Liner notes by Harry Haze

Now, while Harry thinks he's projecting to the world how competent, versatile, and creative he is, I'm thinking, "Harry Haze must be some god-awful prick—an insufferable control freak who can't find anyone crazy enough to work with him."

Uh-oh. Harry Haze has also included a full insert of tiny-printed text: Thank you's to various celestial deities, departed family members, a current wife, an ex-girlfriend, and a deceased pet. Gratitude is a lovely quality best saved for a commercial release. On a demo (in my opinion) such grandiose sentiments seem self-serving and off-putting.

Everything is a reflection of the music. Cheesy cover art often mirrors what is contained within, but words are equally revealing. Vague and self-aggrandizing terms such as. "prestigious," "long-awaited," "eagerly anticipated," or "acclaimed" never fail to rev up my B.S. meter. Also, please have a competent proofreader check your printed materials and your CD covers for glaring errors.

The best packages are often the most simple. A clean, distinctive logo, a smart, well-written bio in a readable, eye-catching font, and a hip, revealing photo say much more than simply seeing the artist's name repeated ad infinitum.

I don't wish to sound negative or jaded, but as the packages pile up in my office, my eyes become ever more critical. I'm reminded that when we project our music into the world, —propelling our artistry out there—we're in essence cramming messages into bottles. When they ultimately wash up on a journalistic shore, we shouldn't let an incompetent presentation sink the package.

The Man in the Gorilla Suit

Recall the '80s—an era of excess, success, and unabashed consumerism? In those pre-DIY days, record conglomerates flourished, and the perception was that in order to become successful as a recording artist, one had to be signed to a major label.

Artists and their representatives would go to unparalleled lengths to get the attention of record company A&R reps, showering them with gifts, appearing unannounced in their foyers singing *a capella*, and devising extravagant presentation packages.

One of my favorite stories from that time concerns a band who was so desperate to get attention that one of the band members donned a gorilla suit to deliver their package to the record company. Today, I don't recall the name of the band or their music. All I can remember—and I'm sure the poor A&R guy does, if this didn't drive him out of the business—is the gorilla suit. Yes, it's important to get people's attention in entertainment, but you want people to remember you for the right reasons.

Extreme Strategies

I told this story to a class of students in England who were amazed at my audacity. I was managing an artist affiliated with a performing rights organization. There was one exec in particular who we believed would make a tremendous ally, and since he was someone I knew, I began making calls to his office to set up a meeting for my client. I left repeated messages, but I wasn't getting a return call. (In his defense, let me interject that the employees of PROs are tremendously challenged by their huge membership rosters—hundreds of thousands of affiliates.) Still, I needed this hookup.

I created a relationship with his sympathetic assistant. When I called one morning, I didn't ask for him, I spoke only to her. "What's his day like?" I asked. She replied, "He's in meetings this morning, he has a lunch appointment, and then more meetings this afternoon." I casually asked what restaurant he'd be dining in for lunch, and she provided the name of a well-known Sunset Strip eatery. That was all I needed to hear. That afternoon, as he paid his bill at the restaurant cash register, guess who just happened to run into him? I had an opportunity to reintroduce my client; he apologized for not calling back and promised to meet with us the next day. In this case, the "chance encounter" had to appear natural and accidental, otherwise it may have seemed as if I was a stalker—not a good thing.

I have another secret weapon I utilize when it's appropriate, albeit a very small one—my four-pound Chihuahua, Shelby Lynne. She has accompanied me to drop off materials, for brief meetings, and on one memorable occasion, backstage to visit a well-known diva who was considering having me ghostwrite her autobiography. I didn't get that gig, but not because of the dog. I wasn't flying blind—this singer was a well-known pet advocate who traveled worldwide with her own pooch.

If you utilize an extreme tactic, you have to be sure you have the goods; otherwise, you're in danger of burning a bridge. Above all, don't be the guy in the gorilla suit.

Rejection

Rejection is a cold, hard fact in the entertainment business. For songwriters and artists in particular, it can be a crushing and demoralizing reality. Indeed, it is often cited as a factor that forces people out of the entertainment business. And this is a good thing: It leaves more room for you. In order to be successful on any level, you can't let rejection derail you. The classic example of the Beatles, who were turned down by scores of record labels, is one of the best-known tales.

It's difficult for anyone to turn down anything, however, if its viability has being proven. An artist who is touring, has a solid fan base, and can sell a few thousand CDs doesn't have to worry about rejection—it's momentary, because they're already a viable commodity. Songwriters who are collaborating with artists, placing songs in indie films and on cable television shows, will be more likely to be signed by a major publishing company because they already have it going on.

Hit songwriter Michéle Vice-Maslin notes that while writers can be discouraged by rejection letters, she is not. "I probably have 25,000. Who cares? I think the key to surviving—other than pitching—is respecting other people's opinions. The A&R people like to deal with me because I don't freak out. As long as they keep listening, I'm happy. I learned once again: Don't give up. It's a lesson I've been learning the hard way for over 20 years. The more I get rejected, the more I get fueled."

Ten Thoughts on Overcoming Rejection

Keep the following in mind when you experience rejection.

1. If someone rejects your song, they are not negating or condemning your existence on this earth.

2. "No" can mean "not at this time," "not for this artist," or "not in this market."

3. In Los Angeles, especially, industry people don't like to say "no." They just won't call you back.

4. You have to develop a career on multiple contacts, numerous outlets, and a catalog of songs. If you have one song you're shopping and you're "waiting to hear back," you're in a precarious position.

5. No one is ever really "waiting to hear back." You have to move forward, regardless.

6. Ironically, projects often succeed when we least need or expect them to.

7. Holding grudges over rejection is counterproductive.

8. It's understandable that songwriters in particular are emotionally connected to their creations. Remember: If a publisher says "no," how many times has a label, artist, or producer said the same thing to him?

9. You are much more likely to be rejected if you're blindly pitching to strangers.

10. As salesmen know, every rejection is one more step toward someone saying "yes."

Ten Reasons Your Calls Are Not Returned

Sometimes it's difficult to have perspective on what we're doing wrong in our communication with others. Often, it may have nothing to do with us *per se*; it could simply be an issue of timing. Following is an e-mail I received that made me analyze why some calls are returned and others aren't.

Dear Dan,

Last year I had the good fortune to meet a major record producer at a music business convention. In a listening session, he evaluated my demo, which he liked enough to keep. But he hasn't returned my calls. I wonder: Am I doing something wrong? Does he feel differently about my music? What would you suggest?

Worried in Winnetka

Following is my response.

Dear Worried,

A number of possible scenarios come to mind.

1. First, do you appear to be too needy? If so, you may be scaring him off. He will take you seriously if you appear to be near, or on your way to, his level of accomplishment.

2. Are you pressuring him? He probably has enough demands in his world from artists, record companies, and associates. He doesn't need them from you.

3. Are you calling at the right time? Professionals call during business hours, not evenings or weekends. Try Tuesdays–Thursdays, preferably before lunch.

4. Are your communication skills up to par? People don't have time to read lengthy communiqués or often to return telephone calls. Short e-mails and faxes are preferable. Check your spelling and sentence structure.

5. The moment that someone hears something is not necessarily the moment they can do something with it. When he listened to your music, he may have recognized its potential but did not have an appropriate outlet at the time. This can change. I've seen songs for films used years after they were first submitted.

6. Make sure to update him on your progress. In fact, you should regularly configure press releases to inform your contacts on your career. But be wary of over-the-top bragging or shameless self-promotion. Keep it to scale, keep it human, keep it true, and make the truth sound as good as possible.

7. In my experience, music business people are always looking for progression; that is, the producer may have indeed liked your first demo, and now he needs to hear what you have next. It will be easier for him to imagine your future career trajectory, and to become involved, if he believes your music will find an audience no matter what.

8. In our business, everyone prefers to get on a train that's up and running, not the one stalled on the tracks. You need to give the impression of growth, of career evolution, of really having something new to say. If we are only reactive—and jump on a bandwagon just because it's there—we will ultimately wind up chasing trends, not creating them.

9. Are you delivering ultimatums? Closed-end phrases will close doors. "Do you want to produce me?" can easily be answered with a "no." Asking for input is always preferable to a hard sell.

10. Finally, are you treating him as a person or as a stepping stone? Are you aware of the projects he's doing now—his successes, career milestones, anything in his life? Try communicating with him in a low-key, personal tone with no "payback" expected. You may be surprised at his response.

I hope this information is helpful. Please let me know how it goes.

Dan Kimpel

Web-Wise

In 1992, when I was the advertising director for the Los Angeles Songwriters Showcase (LASS), our co-founder and director, John Braheny, author of *The Craft and Business of Songwriting* and one of my foremost mentors in the music business, told me about this new technology called the Internet and how he planned to put our organization's magazine, the *Songwriters Musepaper*, up on the Web. I recall thinking to myself, "But who is going to ever see that?"

Time has, of course, proven J.B. right. Tracks legally downloaded from the Internet now outsell physical singles. There were a record 312,000 legal downloads in the final week of 2004, compared with 282,000 singles bought over the counter during the same week. The Internet is *the* watershed for business in music, an incredibly empowering medium for an independent artist. Just as with home recording, by which you no longer need a truck full of money and Abbey Road to make a cool recording because you can create great sounding, personal work in your bedroom, similarly, you no longer need a middle man to deliver your product direct to your audience. You now have the Internet. The barriers to access don't exist anymore.

Do I Need a Web Site?

Doesn't everyone? My personal site (www.dankimpel.com) was designed for me by one of my outstanding students from the Liverpool Institute for Performing Arts, Simon Barber. A musician, band leader, and songwriter, Simon is also a savvy Web master with his own company, Juicing Room (www.juicingroom.com), that specializes in entertainment clients.

Every objection I had to instigating my own site was easily overcome by Simon in a meeting over coffee in England, and soon I too had a great way for folks worldwide to find me. For this section of *Networking Strategies*, I decided to tap Simon's expertise since he now lectures on the subject.

DK: *Give us a little overview.*

SB: Arming yourself with knowledge of how to operate on the Web can allow you to forge a career without waiting for a benevolent benefactor to approve of your talent. If you're Web-phobic, you should know that there's really no escape from the Web. You need to embrace it; make that your mantra. For me, a band/artist needs a Web site just as soon as they are trying to build a fan base. It's the ideal, low-cost way to communicate with fans, advertise gigs, sell CDs, and generally promote.

Many bands assume that if they're good, they'll get picked up by a major label, and that will take care of all the hard graft involved with being an indie. As you know, getting signed does not guarantee getting famous, getting your CD in stores, or getting paid! Over 30,000 CDs are released each year, mainly from people you've never heard of, and only 1% ever sells over 1,000 units. It's really the grassroots kind of operations that are finding and developing talent effectively, especially on a local level.

DK: *What are the economic ramifications for indie artists?*

SB: If you're an independent using the Internet as your means of distribution, you can have anything between 50% and 100% share of the revenue from a product. You may not have access to the large distribution networks or the marketing muscle of major corporations, but you do have a worldwide platform with zero overhead. So, keep costs down and maximize profit. If you can sell 5,000 CDs for $15, that's a lot of money! Far more than you would get with a 12% royalty rate when you're unrecouped and won't earn a penny until you go double platinum. If that ever happens! Plus, with indie budgets, nobody is going to be bankrupt if it doesn't work out. It's not like you're Microsoft and you just rolled out a product all over the country and then realized it's defective. You still have time to grow as an artist, a concept that the bottom line of major labels can no longer afford.

DK: *How did you get into it yourself?*

SB: I formed an independent label called Digital Wings. The label was founded on the philosophy I had of using new technology as a means of liberating new artists from the traditional shackles of the industry.

We released an album called *Motion Picture* with my band Santa Carla, and we built up quite a following on the Web. The year that the record came out, 2003, we had almost two million visitors to the Web site. This was down to a combination of good Web promotion and good search engine work. If you want to effectively drive traffic to a site, you need to do three things.

1. Use good meta tags and make good submissions to the likes of DMOZ. (See the reference list at the end of this chapter.)
2. Siphon traffic from more popular Web sites (MP3, CD Baby) to your personal site by putting up a few free tracks, a photo, and a link to you.
3. Update regularly!

By doing this, we were able to keep a percentage of these fans on mailing lists for marketing new releases to, and of course, some of them visited the site daily to post messages.

We got some excellent press from America and did some international radio sessions. It did well in the end and sold a couple of thousand copies, too. We made it available in all the indie stores, and we did a series of free downloads at digital music services across the Web. It's available to buy online at iTunes, CDWOW, Tower Records, and other credible retailers who support independent artists. So through using the Net, we were able to do two UK tours for the album and actually have these people show up at the gigs like a pre-booked audience. It's about self-sufficiency. If you're prepared to sweat for your art, then it's a very effective way to operate.

DK: *Give us some hard facts and numbers regarding setting up a site.*

SB: The costs of setting up are not prohibitive at all. You might be looking at $20–$25 for a domain and maybe $75 a year for hosting.

DK: *OK, it sounds easy and inexpensive so far, but your perspective is as a Web designer. What can you tell us about making the site alluring to visitors?*

SB: If you're not up to it, find someone with a good sense of graphics, fonts, and layout. Someone who understands functionality and the basic commandments of the Web so that you don't end up with a style-over-substance situation. It is very easy to spot home-made Web sites that have poor functionality, use entry-level gimmicks, have poor color schemes, unreadable text, or do not validate on different browsers/platforms.

Your Web site should

▶   Get a user's e-mail address.
▶   Offer easy ways to listen to the artist.
▶   Make the product attractive to them.
▶   Show who are you, what you look like, and most important, what you sound like.
▶   Acknowledge and interact with visitors.

Music clips should be presented in a cross-platform format such as MP3. Avoid proprietary formats where possible. People don't really buy music for the audio, they buy the whole package. Make it an exciting pic that says something about you and who you are. Include a bio. Get an angle and tie it in with the photo and tell the visitor what you represent.

Create a mailing list, a viable way to harvest data from your visitors. Find out as much as possible about the fans: age, location (especially if it's a town you're playing in), etc. What sort of music do they like and what Web sites do they visit? What lists do they subscribe to at stores they visit online? See if your CD is stocked there. As an indie, you need to manage your own contact list and get used to the idea of staying in contact with large groups of people at any one time.

You'll also need to create an easy and effective way to merchandise and a way for fans to buy your CDs. Remember, people are infinitely more interested in themselves than they are in you. Put them on your site with message boards. Use it to create a street team. Don't forget that to most people, the music business is pure magic—put your fan base to work.

DK: *Are there key sites that should be utilized?*

SB: CD Baby (www.cdbaby.com) is the root of many great indie options—a selling point with built-in traffic, digital distribution services, Tower Records, etc.

Become aware of your local network and what's going on, who the local bands are, what they're doing, and where they're playing.

DK: *Any other valuable promo tools we should be aware of?*

SB: An electronic press kit with at least one full-length MP3 file of a track from your CD encoded at the standard 128K bit rate. An entertaining bio written four times, in four different lengths, quotes from reviews, plus graphics, artist photos, cover art, and your logo.

Additional Resources

www.coolhomepages.com Cool Home Pages, an excellent design resource.

www.coolhomepages.com/cda/10commandments Ten Commandments of Design; an interesting article on the subject.

www.google.com Google; the search engine you need to show up in.

www.dmoz.com DMOZ; human-edited search engine.

www.phpbb.com PHPBB; message board software.

www.hostbaby.com Hostbaby; Web hosting for musicians.

www.jetplanelanding.com Jetplane Landing; an excellent independent band with a powerful site.

www.santacarla.co.uk Santa Carla's site.

www.juicingroom.com Juicing Room; a Web company.

www.digitalwings.co.uk Digital Wings; a record label.

www.apple.com/itunes/store Apple iTunes.

www.napster.co.uk Napster.

ww.listen.com Rhapsody.

www.peoplesound.com Peoplesound.

www.garageband.com Garageband.

www.towerrecords.com Tower Records.

www.cdwow.com CDWOW.

www.cdbaby.com CD Baby.

www.fopp.co.uk/unsigned_network/intro.htm Fopp Unsigned.

www.cafepress.com Café Press; music merchandise.

www.gigwise.com Gigwise; local music community.

www.glasswerk.co.uk Glasswerk; local music community.

www.bbc.co.uk/liverpool/entertainment/music/unsigned_bands/index.shtml BBC Unsigned; valuable promotion tool.

www.musicbias.org Musicbias; local music business support.

www.marketingyourmusic.com Marketing Your Music (by the genius behind CD Baby).

www.bob-baker.com Bob Baker; marketing tips.

www.getsigned.com Get Signed.

CHAPTER 8

Live Venues and Ventures

The heart of popular music beats within the live performance. Even if you are not engaged in a career as a performer, odds are you're working with those who are. In this chapter, you'll go backstage with the band.

Gigology 101

Since I live in Los Angeles, it would be possible for me to go out 365 nights a year, hit 10 clubs every night, and never see even a tiny fraction of what's happening in town. Given these exhaustive possibilities, it is unnerving when I am invited by some well-meaning band to come by a club at 11:00 P.M. on a Monday night to catch their set. I'm more apt to be at home in flannel pajamas, watching the news with a Chihuahua dog on my lap at this hour, resting up for the day ahead. This is not to say that I don't go out, but I have to measure the importance of the shows I attend. I'm more likely to go out if a friend is performing, it's a band I'm passionate about, because

I'm writing something about the act, or because the networking possibilities are promising.

The worst time to showcase in a major music city is on weekends. This may be when the rank and file go out to party, but in my experience, music industry professionals prefer to reserve their personal weekend time for their families. For them, hearing bands is hard work; it's what they do for a living. And no one wants to work all of the time. For these busy professionals, weeknights are preferable, and an early show, where they can come directly from the office, is ideal.

All of us in the industry have clubs where we prefer to see artists—where the sight lines are favorable, the sound pristine, the staff professional and accommodating. And of course the opposite is true: I would rather chew glass than go to another show at a certain Hollywood club (formerly owned by a famous actor) because the staff is invariably rude, officious, and makes me feel like a criminal when they search me.

Creative Outlets

There is a certain mystique, historical and otherwise, attached to places like The Troubadour in Los Angeles, the Bitter End in New York, and The Bluebird in Nashville. I present this theory: Audiences respond to entertainment in direct correlation to the environment in which they see it. This is a reason that the mediocre entertainment accompanied by laser and light shows wows the masses in Las Vegas—the audience has been set up by the surroundings. Conversely, seeing the greatest band in the world in a sleazy club may not necessarily

showcase their brilliance, because the seamy circumstances have prepared the audience for something less.

At one point in my career in Los Angeles, I was
promoting a vocal trio with a very original sound—a
Manhattan Transfer meets Carter Family vibe, with an
intricate, delicate blend, far too subtle for a club environment. I met with all three members of the band for
dinner one night at a modest Japanese restaurant with
'50s decor, including turquoise and pink walls, and black
and white checked floors. As we devoured our California
rolls, the trio's leader began bemoaning the lack of a
perfect venue. "What about here?" I asked. They looked
at me as if the wasabi had gone to my brain. We were in
a restaurant, not a club, a venue that didn't even have
music. "Perfect," I deduced.

Later that week I wrote up a proposal and
approached the restaurant's owners with a guaranteed
way for them to bring in people and make money one
evening at their busy daytime location that had sparse
dinner business. We would produce a music night,
bringing in production staff and a sound system, charge
a cover at the door that would go to the band, and the
restaurant could serve their regular food, drinks, and
desserts and profit from these sales. When the evening of
the performance arrived, the venue was packed—so full,
in fact, that the restaurant's wait staff panicked, and our
friends had to help serve the food, but the group made
over $1,000 at the door, and the evening had a huge buzz
that carried over to successive shows.

Next, I booked the trio into small theaters for
weekend matinee performances. Since the band's
setup was minimal and acoustic, they could work

around a preexistent set and not disturb the physical elements of the evening's performances. In Los Angeles, we have equity-waver houses (99 seats or less) that we could sell out on a Saturday afternoon. We also provided concessions and merchandise, upping the take considerably.

Alternative Venues

Creative new venues can work with multiple artists as well. I was managing a performer who had devised a world-influenced brand of pop music. When we decided it was time to take the music to the stage, we couldn't find an adequate venue, so we decided to invent our own. To complement his global grooves, we invited two other acts with whom we were friendly: A Latin band from East Los Angeles and a roots reggae group.

I located an appropriate venue, an historic women's club in Los Angeles, and convinced the directors that I was creating an event of cultural significance. I set up sponsorships with magazines, a music store, and a sound company, so I wasn't paying out of pocket for anything other than the venue. Tickets were affordable, and I made each of the three acts (my own included) responsible for selling a set number so we were assured of a full house. The bands would make a profit after their initial sale, and they could also move merchandise plus have a high-profile showcase concert with media attention.

I will always recall standing in the parking lot with a trio of matronly women from the club's board of directors when the reggae group arrived for sound check, and the looks on their faces as five hugely dreadlocked musicians emerged through the clouds of pungent smoke that billowed from their van. Jah! Rastafari! The evening was a huge success.

Inventing Your Own Show

Consider the following tips if you plan to create your own show.

1. Give the show a name. Our global music show was titled "World Tribe."

2. Create a logo and artwork specific to the venue.

3. Think way outside the box. I've been to art galleries, fashion shows, and pet rescue events to hear bands.

4. Write up your proposal; business people always respond better when something is in print.

5. Consider a residency, or an ongoing show for one designated night per week, but keep in mind there is a natural lifespan to such events. Know when it's time to move on.

Soft Ticket

With one artist, I thought big—of having him perform to audiences of more than 10,000 people. The reality was that he was from Hawaii, hadn't yet made an impact on the mainland, and had no reputation to speak of, so it was up to me to devise a way to present him in front of as many people as possible. A "soft ticket" refers to an event that people are attending already—a fair, a festival—where they will see the entertainment as well. It can be a perfect opportunity for a high-visibility show.

I approached the entertainment committee for an annual Asian-Pacific celebration in Los Angeles that draws thousands of visitors. I proposed presenting my artist and, as an added incentive, offered to provide publicity and public relations services for the event free of charge. I was able to "piggy-back" my artist's appearance on top of the event and to make it appear (subtly, of course) as if he were headlining. Through press, stories, publicity, and media saturation, we were able to create a significant splash.

How to Make a Soft Ticket Show Work for You

Consider the following tips for creating your soft ticket show.

1. Research the demographics; you don't want to present a nu-metal band at a gathering of senior citizens.

2. Write up your proposal, focusing on what you or your artist can do for the event, not vice-versa.

3. Play for expenses or even for free if necessary. Make your money in merchandise sales or write-off expenses for the value of publicity.

4. Outdoor shows are not a place for ballads—devise a high energy, visually engaging show that will make those in attendance stop to watch you.

5. Create a banner with the name of your band on it and hang it at outdoor events (or anywhere else you play). "Who is that band?" is not a question that your audience should walk away asking.

You Sounded Fabulous!

Accepting compliments seems to be difficult for many performers. I attended a wonderful showcase in Liverpool, England, with one of my students. After the set, I went backstage to congratulate her. "You were terrific!" I enthused.

"Nah, the sound was awful, I couldn't hear the monitors, and I forgot some lyrics," was her mumbled response.

Maybe she was being honest, and of course that's commendable in most circumstances, but this is show business. By denigrating a performance on which I'd complimented her, she was unconsciously criticizing my taste and therefore undercutting my enjoyment of the show.

Ten Post-Performance Tips

1. Be gracious, accept compliments, and thank the person who gives them.

2. Remember, non-music people are often less critical, enjoying the overall gestalt of a show and often not noticing the mistakes.

3. Don't call attention to negative conditions in the club.

4. Always graciously thank those who spent good money and came to see you perform.

5. If you're hanging out in a club after the performance, don't hop from table to table. Stay in one location and let the audience members come to you.

6. Sign everything. Often fans will pay more for a CD signed by the artist in person than they would at retail or online. I've worked with artists who mark $15 CDs up to $20 at shows and sell hundreds. Audiences will pay for the opportunity to meet the artist.

7. If you're selling merchandise, don't handle the money yourself, enlist help.

8. Have plenty of Sharpies or similar pens on hand.

9. Be prudent in handing out promotional materials for upcoming performances that are in venues other than the one in which you've just appeared. The club owner may frown on your promotion of a competing venue.

10. Cover your show clothes with a jacket, or change into another outfit immediately after the performance.

Performance Peeves

I'm mystified why I see so many musicians swilling bottled water onstage. "Is this a show about water?" I wonder. I understand a singer taking a swig to combat dryness, but why is everyone else draining the Aquafina?

At an otherwise splendid show, a musical tribute to Joni Mitchell, I could predict what was about to be performed because the lead guitarist would play the intro lick to check his tone before each song. Surprise is good in performance; don't telegraph what's coming, and don't use "weedlee, weedlee" licks when the singer is introducing the song. Just as music is rehearsed, so should the intros and outros be a part of the overall performance. Dull, self-conscious stage patter detracts from a performance. The song intro is a chance to connect on another level.

Ten Commandments of Club Land

1. Don't piss off the soundman; that's just asking for endless feedback and appalling apathy.

2. Respect the club booker; she will eventually be at House of Blues.

3. Be honest about your draw. If you can only guarantee 10 close friends for attendance, don't proclaim that you can fill a 500-seat venue.

4. "We're gonna slow it down for ya now" is not a suitable song intro.

5. Don't rail against any member of the press or threaten any music journalist.

6. Speak well of other bands on the circuit. You'll be on a bill with them sooner or later.

7. Be unerringly professional and punctual.

8. A sound check is not a rehearsal.

9. Be conscientious with your guest list. Don't demand freebies from the club.

10. Devise original ways of filling the venue.

Club Clues

With the goal of selling as many drinks as possible, clubs are businesses, plain and simple. If your goal is to be a club act, that's fine, but at some point you'll have to determine whether you're in the music business or the bar business and act accordingly. As a musician, I made a decent living playing in clubs in tough markets, including New York and Los Angeles. In order to do this, however, I was forced to make many concessions in my art. Even though I wrote songs, it was a rare audience who wanted to party to unheard-of material, so covers were the way to go. There is a certain vibe that club musicians acquire. It's difficult to describe, but audiences can feel it. (You can read Bob Malone's comments about his own experiences in this realm in Chapter 9, "Success Stories.") You are in the realm of service.

There are, of course, exceptions to this rule. Coming up with a band in Ohio, we transformed a club in the college town of Bowling Green—Howard's Club H—into a Mecca for free-thinking individuals of all persuasions. In Los Angeles, a club called Limey's hosted the hippest ever musician's Sunday night jam. But these scenes are few and far between. And if you perform in the same clubs over and over again, you're in danger of becoming part of the furniture because careers are built on change and progression. It doesn't take audiences very long to begin to take you for granted. If you're comfortable at the same club, it's probably time to move on.

Soundman Scenarios

In my list above, I cautioned you about angering the soundman. There are many intricacies in dealing with technical personnel. Doing their gig is often a thankless job accompanied by a howl of feedback, a singer complaining "I can't hear myself," mics that don't work, and monitors that fail to deliver. If the sound is terrible, it's the soundman's fault and, of course, if it's flawless no one notices. Consequently, soundmen (and women) tend to be a prickly lot, often either over-sensitive or immune to criticism, since they deal with a new band virtually every night, always with a new raft of complaints.

It's an excellent idea to always have a hard copy depiction of your set-up: mic and monitor placements and an input list. E-mailing or faxing this information to the club ahead of time if possible, or having this information on your Web site, can save time and energy. Take multiple copies to your sound check in case there is a stage manager in addition to the soundman. If the club provides a backline (drums, amps, etc.), all the better.

If there are multiple acts for a show, the band who is playing last, or headlining, typically sound checks first. The group who opens the show sound checks last since their equipment can then be in place when the doors open. Being on time for the sound check is the first objective, since sound checks invariably run late. Do everyone a favor and have the band arrive together.

Here's a scenario that works extremely well for me when I present artists in a club or concert. I stay in the sound booth as the soundman adjusts levels in the line check (each instrument heard individually) and as the band runs down a song. At this point I don't say a word to the soundman, I am simply a strong and obvious presence hovering next to the board. Invariably the soundman will then solicit my opinion. The secret is to stay mum and await this moment. It will come, I assure you. Then, and only then, gently correct any miscalculations in the mix.

Always thank the soundman—either onstage, immediately after the performance, or in a note or e-mail the next day. Be sure to let the booker or club owner know how much you've appreciated the hard work and expertise of the technical staff at the venue. The sound and stage personnel will be glad to see you next time.

Scams

Envision this scenario. You see a solicitation in a magazine from a company that is reviewing the type of music you create. You send in your package and—surprise!—you receive a call from a company executive who praises your efforts and proclaims that your music is in the top percentile of what he has ever received. It is *so* stunning that he would love to have the opportunity to represent this wondrous music to the major players: the big markets, radio, record companies, etc. In fact, your music is *so* magnificent that he will even give you a healthy discount on the fees that he usually charges for these services.

At this point, a red light begins flashing in your brain. "Money? I have to pay money?" you say. The eloquent one then ups the intensity of his fevered pitch, "You have to spend money to make money. I've worked with (insert platinum artist here) and (insert another platinum artist here), and I'm respected in this business for hearing the hits. I believe in your music; I can make it happen for you."

The music business is filled with inventive cottage industries. However, charging naive acts exorbitant fees to "shop" their material is a gray area where I've seen many an aspiring artist turn into bleeding bait for the circling sharks.

There is, for instance, one Hollywood-based "promoter" who turns a pretty profit by luring artists into his gold record-decorated den and then pressuring them to pay for his services. His pitch rarely wavers: He is, in the next three days, traveling to New York (a convenient 3,000 miles away) and has meetings already set up to play material for the heads of major record labels. This takes money. The up-front fee? $8,000.

When I was on the staff of a national non-profit organization for songwriters, I encountered numerous victims of this particular scamster. Many were reticent to complain because, like most scam victims, they were mortified by their own gullibility.

If you're ever approached by anyone in the business with a sketchy proposition, I would advise the following:

1. First and foremost, trust your instincts.

2. Ask them for the names and contact numbers of clients.

3. Request additional industry references.

4. Check them out online. There's a site called The Velvet Rope (www.thevelvetrope.com) where, if you are a member, you can post industry-related queries. If you prefer, you can remain anonymous while asking, "Has anyone ever worked with...?"

5. Don't assume that the operator is legit just because he advertises in a legitimate music business publication. Some magazines would accept advertising from Satan himself if he paid up front. It's up to you to exert your judgment.

6. The music business is very small. Bottom-feeding sleazes depend upon their victims *not* to have information or resources. Don't be afraid to ask for references to verify a company or a person's legitimacy.

7. Keep in mind that there are no shortcuts in the music business. Nothing will ever replace the power of creating your own personal contacts and network.

8. Educate yourself about how the business really works. Don't allow your ego or a sense of desperation to make your decisions for you.

Compilation CDs

OK, emerging bands: You've performed, postered, postured, and proclaimed to the pinnacle of your powers. So now that you're starting to kick up some notice, you've been invited to have a song included on a compilation CD. Sure, it may cost a few hundred dollars, but it will be delivered directly into the hands of radio, record company A&R, promoters, and bookers.

Compilations are wonderful money-making devices for the ones who can persuade 15 to 20 bands to each give them one song and to pay anywhere from $500 to $1000 for the privilege. In turn, the producers master and manufacture a couple of hundred CDs, give some copies to the bands, mail out to their "contacts," and voila, they've pocketed a few grand in the process. And the bands? They have copies of a CD with 19 other groups whose sole shared merit is coming up with the cash to pay for a track.

There are, of course, worthwhile, legitimate compilations. The performing rights societies (ASCAP, BMI, and SESAC) will often showcase emerging bands and writers via a compilation. The Los Angeles–based organization L.A. Women in Music (LAWIM) has a diverse, highly regarded release. But in neither of these scenarios is there any cost to the artists. Likewise, there are worthwhile CD compilations that target specific local scenes or styles of music. These can often reflect an emerging music community and offer an effective way for groups to share the costs of manufacturing, artwork, etc.

Likewise, certain record companies will present their emerging acts on promotional sampler CDs at no cost to the bands. And of course on late-night television one can order everything from heart-wrenching patriotic songs to the nearly forgotten hair bands of the '80s. These artists, even at a reduced royalty, will benefit from the sale of the CDs.

But let's get real. Why should a record label exec listen to 20 disconnected bands on one release? Would a journalist really wade through 19 groups with the hope of hearing something interesting if he had no connection to the producers? Believe this: Radio programmers and record label people, realizing that the criterion for inclusion on compilations is simply whether an artist can pay the fee to be included, will generally disdain such compilations.

One of the latest wrinkles in the well-worn scam is the "event" tie-in. It works like this: "We're going to be at (MIDEM/SXSW/EAT'EM/Sundance/Slamdance), and we'll be distributing CDs to everyone there." Sounds good, but how do you know that the CDs will even be distributed? After all, the point is that you won't be there anyway, will you? And how much baggage might a convention-goer accumulate over a couple of days? And how much do they actually want to take home?

If you're asked to participate in a compilation CD project, here are some questions you should ask the producers.

- ▶ What type of track record do they have in the industry?
- ▶ What acts have been signed from their previous releases?
- ▶ What criteria do they have for inclusion?
- ▶ Do they provide group contact info with the release?
- ▶ Does the group maintain control of the song's copyright?

Ask for their previous releases, then give a good, hard listen to determine if these acts are those with whom you'd like to share CD space. In the music business, the way you come in is the way that you're perceived. Often, being included on a dubious project is almost worse that not being heard at all, especially if you're sandwiched between a couple of lousy groups.

Compilation CDs are wonderfully lucrative endeavors for their producers. But for bands with limited economic resources, being included on a compilation project may only land you on a CD that a record company exec, radio programmer, or journalist reaches for when he needs a coaster for his cocktail.

Performing Rights

If you write songs for your band, you need to choose a performing rights organization. You're in luck because there are three: ASCAP, BMI, and SESAC. All are imminently accessible, and all are (believe it or not) there to help you. As a songwriter, you can affiliate with only one society. On the surface, what these three performing rights organizations (PROs) do is not dissimilar: They collect money for songwriters and music publishers from broadcast revenue sources, including television, radio, and Internet licenses. They then distribute these funds to their members.

Sounds good, right? Keep in mind that you will never receive one penny from these sources if you do not affiliate, which is reason enough to contact them as soon as you have, or anticipate having, a CD that might be receiving any kind of airplay.

ASCAP, the oldest and largest of the three organizations, boasts among their membership many of the most venerated songwriters in the history of pop music. ASCAP Presents showcases unsigned bands in various cities around the U.S. Buckcherry, Lit, Gin Blossoms, and Save Ferris are all alumni. Also among the extensive list of workshops for songwriters is "Music Business 101," informational and educational sessions with guest speakers, and ASCAP SWAPmeet, held in various cities, including L.A., where new works are heard by industry pros. ASCAP, governed by a board of directors elected from their membership, can be reached at (323) 883-1000 or contacted online at www.ascap.com.

BMI, formed as an alternative to ASCAP, originally licensed R&B and country music. Today, they are equally strong in rock and pop. BMI co-sponsors and produces live performance opportunities for members and is involved in many grass-roots events. New Music Nights is a quarterly program on the West coast that showcases a wide variety of genres—rock, alternative, pop, soul and hip-hop— to help expose new talent to the industry—lawyers, managers, A&R, publicists, and journalists, as well to the general public at large. Bands who have played and/or been signed from the showcase include Counting Crows, The Roots, Stroke 9, and Train and Creed. Contact BMI at 310-659-9109 or online at www.bmi.com.

Speaking of alternatives, SESAC, although not as widely known as the other two organizations, is definitely making up for lost time with an aggressive marketing campaign and some key signings. Oscar-winning songwriter, the legendary Bob Dylan, is a SESAC writer. SESAC has made strategic alliances with a host of technology companies and was the first PRO to offer digital watermarking so you're paid every time your song is aired. They also offer online licensing for affiliates and online registration of works. SESAC is a privately held company and is selective about its affiliates. You can reach them in Los Angeles at (310) 393-9671 or online at www.sesac.com.

Which society is right for you? Contact all three then examine the materials they offer concerning payment schedules and contract length. Above all, trust your instincts and remember that having someone who believes in you at a performing rights organization is one major step up the ladder in this business.

CHAPTER 9

Success Stories

In the mythology of the music business, there is a huge focus on the million-selling stars—the bands we see on MTV and VH1—those very few who enjoy their brief moment teetering on the chart-topping pinnacle of success. As I've reiterated in this book, I believe the true success stories are of those individuals who figure out how to work and stay in the business they love, who can remain relevant over time, and who are able to sustain themselves through an art they love.

In this chapter, it's my pleasure to introduce you to some folks whose accomplishments are varied, wide, and enduring. They exemplify networking strategies through their steadfast commitment and determination to find a way to keep themselves in the game. There's a lot to be learned from their career journeys.

Jeffrey Steele: Country Craftsman

With over 200 songs recorded in the last three years by Nashville's most bankable stars, including Tim McGraw, Faith Hill, Montgomery Gentry, Rascal Flatts, Leanne Rimes, and Diamond Rio, Jeffrey Steele is as hot as a country songwriter could possibly be. But songwriting success for this driven Californian came only after two decades of broken dreams, busted-up bands, deals gone sour, and experiences with record executives who thought they knew more about country music than Jeffrey Steele. "The most important thing any songwriter needs to have is that drive, an 'against all odds' instinct to keep writing through all the rejection and all the hardships," states Steele. "These are your stories, the stuff that turns into your songs. I think a lot of people run from these things, but they need to realize that that's what you're gonna be writing about for the next 20 years."

Independent releases sold on his Web site and at live shows have been, up until now, the only way to procure Steele's solo work. Now, *Outlaw,* from Lofton Creek, delivers the power of Jeffrey Steele as an artist backed by the power of major distribution. "We found out that one song of mine was being played on one radio station 120 times a week," says Steele. "The song is called 'Good Year for the Outlaw.' It's an outlaw country station, and this is their theme song. The next thing I know, the song is showing up on the *Billboard* chart completely out of the blue." Of the new record that takes its title from the track, Steele notes, "I finally got a record in the store after eight years of being signed to major record deals and not getting records out. It feels good to have an actual piece of product in the Wal-Marts and Targets."

To promote his record, Steele has been opening shows for Brad Paisley and Keith Urban, with just an acoustic guitar. "You've really got to work," he avows. "I came out for 8,000 people in Connecticut, with throngs of screaming women wanting to see Brad and Keith. I said, 'You guys have no idea who I am, but you know my songs.' The whole place was singing along, then I did the stuff from my new record, and '20 Years Ago' earned a standing ovation. But the stage manager wouldn't let me go back out for an encore. So I'm getting success and shooting myself in the foot at the same time. It's all perfect."

Born in Burbank, the youngest of five children, Steele's powers of perception were honed early on. "I observed my older brothers and sisters and heard all of their music," recalls the songwriter. "I was at the bottom end of the food chain, just eating that stuff up, watching and learning. Later, all of these things were there to write about." As the little brother, Steele learned how to vie for attention. "I remember being five, shaking my hips to Elvis Presley records in front of the whole family, and my brothers getting pissed and beating me up later."

One familial theme Steele has referenced in both "My Town" (Montgomery Gentry) and "20 Years Ago" is the age-old conflict between father and son. "It was my brother and my father," he says. " I'd watch them fight at the dinner table. They could never get along. Ten or 15 years went by and they didn't talk to each other until my dad was on his deathbed in a morphine-induced state. They couldn't really make amends, but they could look each other in the eye one last time. I tell writers, 'Don't turn the other way from that. It's OK to write about it more than once, if that's a big issue in your life. It's therapy for you.'"

Twenty years ago thought I knew it all
Trying to talk to me was like taking to a wall
I thought I was a man for acting like I did
But what I want right now is just to be your kid
Just before my dad gave up the ghost
he smiled at me and said
Son let it go, that was 20 years ago.

Steele spent the '80s with a dual music career, playing in bands on the Sunset Strip and with country groups far from the center of L.A. It was in the country bars that he could make a living, but he decided to concentrate on writing songs. Still, he couldn't resist an offer of $200 to play bass one Sunday afternoon. "I put my amp in the car and drove down to Orange Country and played the gig with Larry Parks and his brother Cary, with Hugh Wright on drums. I said, 'These guys are unbelievable.' Next thing I know we're playing every bar in town. I started bringing my songs in, and the harmonies were great. It was a once-in-a-lifetime thing." Boy Howdy's huge radio hit, "She'd Give Anything," took the band to the top of the country charts.

But the record company wanted more of the same, and the band wasn't amenable to being squeezed into the polished Nashville mold. Jeffrey Steele tells of the harrowing days after Boy Howdy's demise, when he was subsequently signed to a solo deal. "I got the worst of the worst, but really no worse than anyone else. When I signed to Curb Records, I remember the guys there telling me all my songs sucked and I wasn't really that talented, but the secretary in the office thought I was cute, so they were going to give me a record deal. All of the things they say to make you feel like nothing." Meanwhile, the publishers were equally underwhelmed. "They told me my songs were nowhere near the market-place—off by a mile. But I knew that I loved to write. It gets to a point where you either slough it off or think maybe they're right. But look at the criticism and see if it has any weight. These guys are critics, and they'll say things to discourage you. Over the years, it's become fire for me."

On this day in Nashville, Jeffrey is behind the board, producing a record on RCA for Keith Anderson, a singer/songwriter he's known for six years who penned "Beer Run" for George Jones and Garth Brooks. "He'd originally gotten a production deal with Sony, and I talked him out of doing it. He said, 'You're going to make it terrible for me. I'm never going to get a deal.' I said, 'No, dude, if you sign a production deal with Sony, you're stuck there. You won't have the option to play for anybody else. We'll pay the money for the first couple of tracks, get everybody interested, and we'll get them all out to see you.' He showcased and had every label in town champing at the bit. Six years ago, he was too left of center."

Between the promotional tours for his record and production gigs, Steele tightly structures his songwriting time. "It's not unusual for me to have three writing appointments a day, like I'm in a doctor's office. People say, 'How can you do anything artistic when you're writing that much?' First of all, I'm a freak. That answers that question," laughs Steele. If his first appointment of the day is productive, it inspires him for the next two sessions and keeps his adrenaline running until the late hours. "I know there's something wrong with me, when I can't shut my brain down, when I'm getting up and writing at three in the morning. I want to keep practicing my lyric craft, get as good as I can. I want to use less words to say more things. Instead of having two lines, I try to get it down to two words."

To the uninitiated, it may be a mystery why Jeffrey Steele, BMI's Songwriter of the Year and one of Nashville's most prolific talents, chooses to tour the hinterlands instead of luxuriating in town, writing songs, and checking the mailbox for what must presumably be formidable checks. He explains that touring stirs his creativity: "Particularly in the small towns, people come up and invariably tell you about their lives, about their cousins, uncles, or talk about something that happened in town. There's something to be said for playing for three hours and sitting in that autograph line for two. I always give everybody the time of day, let them tell me what they tell me. I like to say something positive, make the most of the time. They're happy to see me, and I'm happy to be there. A lot of people get burned out, but I get stories and titles."

He gives this example of a song he co-wrote with Marv Green, the writer of Lonestar's hit, "Amazed." "I was on the autograph line and this guy comes up and he introduces me to his wife, this beautiful lady, and I could tell they're deeply in love. He says, 'She could have had anyone in school.' I said, 'What did you do to get her?' and he said, 'All's I did was love her.' My mental memory bank went on and we wrote the song a couple of days ago. It's about what he talked about—he never had any riches, but he promised her a life of his being there and being good to her."

Steele reveals that he's always prepared to write. "That's what anyone will say, even if I'm an hour late to the writing session. It's because I'm at home working on an idea. I want a seed or something to go on. Putting in 30 to 40 minutes a day playing, trying to think of something, keeps you in that mode all of the time, ready to write something. Even if it's crappy stuff, you're letting your thoughts out. But I hope when a new guy comes in he's also armed and dangerous, is focused, has a bunch of stuff, and wants to write hit songs." Steele shares that sometimes co-writers will expect him to, in his words, "lay a golden egg." He explains, "That's the hardest part—when someone's looking at me going, 'When is it going to happen?' And I'm like, 'When is what going to happen?' If I intend to lay a golden egg, I'm going to do it in the privacy of my home. I'm not going to do it in front of you, pal."

Lindy Robbins: Late Bloomer

These are productive times for Los Angeles songwriter Lindy Robbins. She's penned two songs, "Shine" and "I Will Carry You," for Clay Aiken's platinum debut, *Measure of a Man*; she has a cut with Jesse McCartney on the Disney soundtrack and in the film *Cinderella Story*; she's renegotiated a new publishing pact with media powerhouse Universal Music Publishing Group; and she's preparing to move into a home she's purchased in the San Fernando Valley's trendy NoHo Arts district.

Make no mistake, Lindy Robbins is no overnight success. A native Angeleno who relocated to New York City in the '80s, Robbins' tale is one of fate, faith, trust, and timing. "It was only two years ago that I had any money at all," she confesses. "I was a late bloomer. I had a publishing deal in 1994 with Rodgers and Hammerstein Music in New York, but I was writing theatrical, cabaret, and art songs and making a living performing. It wasn't until 1997 that I quit performing and decided I wanted to write pop songs. I moved back to L.A. to do that, without a deal, without any money, without anything."

On a fluke, she entered a song in the UniSong International Song Contest and won the grand prize. She was subsequently invited to Ireland for Celtic Harmony, a week-long songwriter retreat organized by Music Bridges (USA) in conjunction with Irish rights society IMRO, where she was cast in intensive writing sessions with hit makers from around the world. "I had moved back to L.A. with not a fork," laughs Robbins, "and there I was, onstage, singing with Lamont Dozier and Brenda Russell. It all happened so fast."

In Ireland, Robbins met Rowana Gillespie of Polygram Music Publishing, who signed her to a deal. (The company has since merged with Universal Music Publishing Group.) In addition to a music publisher, Robbins retains the services of a manager. Still, she never stops hustling up her own opportunities. "No matter what cuts you have, you can never stop working your songs," she emphasizes. She makes regular trips to New York to meet personally with A&R executives at various labels. "I've found that if I make a connection, they'll listen to a song later," she explains. "We talk about life for a second. It's a human thing."

Robbins earned serious Music City credentials with a Faith Hill cut, "Back to You," and international recognition for "I Dreamed of You," a four and a half million-seller co-written and recorded by dance diva Anastacia. Unless she is co-writing with an artist, she does not generally write songs with a specific performer in mind, and she cautions writers about becoming what she terms "genre whores." She explains, "Sometimes there are certain types of songs on the radio. You try to copy that trend, and by the time you're shopping those songs, the trend has changed. By the time you're pitching yours, A&R execs have heard a hundred of those songs, and they want to hear something different. Sometimes you have to start the trend yourself." She shares that on many occasions, it's necessary to turn off the business mind in order to create. "It's like, 'Can we just write a great song today?' Sometimes you have to flow and not think about business—just write. And those are the songs that get cut, because they're fun."

A global perspective is vital for pop songwriters, says Robbins. "I've had great things in the U.S., like Clay Aiken and Faith Hill, but I've gotten by on stuff in England, France, and Australia. It's important to investigate other avenues rather than just the U.S. I can go to London and write dance or pop, then go to Nashville and write country, then to New York to write urban. That's what keeps it fresh." Robbins' ability to work quickly makes for a burgeoning catalog. "I can do a song a day easily," she avows. "When I'm on a writing trip I'll do 10 to 15 songs. If 20 percent of them get placed, that makes a huge difference." She writes both melodies and lyrics, and she generally prefers to write with a producer. "I don't work with other writers, except when I'm doing standards or country," she affirms.

Robbins notes that production is key to getting cuts. "That's the biggest lesson I had to learn. As good as some of my songs were, the tracks weren't good enough and the songs wouldn't get placed. The demos have to sound as good as records." Robbins says that it is common practice now for songwriters to create the words and music and then share a 20-percent writing credit with a producer to craft the definitive track. "It's worth it. Without a great demo, a song can't get placed."

In the mercantile world of high-stakes songwriting, Robbins testifies that regular trips to Music City keep her centered. "When I get burnt on writing to tracks, I go to Nashville and get in a room with a great collaborator who plays piano or guitar. All my training in theater and cabaret comes into play there more than anywhere else. With country songs you can be funny and clever. In pop you can't be as poetic. I love Nashville. They've opened their arms at the Universal office—and that Faith Hill cut didn't hurt."

One recent trend that Robbins observes is that country is reverting to a rootsier style. "I'm a Valley Girl," she laughs, "I can't relate as much to the whole Southern experience. I try to write about what I know. But that's what I love about collaboration. If I write with somebody who really understands that, they can help me express it. If I'm writing something urban, I'll only write with someone who understands that world. That expands me. Where I excel is pop rock, so people will bring me in because of my expertise. By finding collaborators who do something different than what I do, I get a lot more versatility in my catalog."

One of her newest collaborators is pop-meister David Frank, a writer/producer probably best known for "Genie in a Bottle," the song that launched the career of

Christina Aguilera. "David and I have just clicked; we're on the same page creatively. The first thing we wrote together got cut by a new artist, Bree Larson. I've found that helps. If you write with someone and get an immediate response to your collaboration, that's encouraging. There might be someone you've written seven songs with and none of them have gotten cut. You have to think maybe it's not the best situation." Ease and comfort in the creative process is another collaborative plus. "Sometimes you have to give it more than one shot, but I'm the type of person who likes to go with something and not think about it. If someone keeps saying 'No, that's not it' and interrupts the flow, then I just want to go home. It should always be fun."

Robbins' writing tools are simple: a spiral notebook, a pen, a rhyming dictionary, a thesaurus, and a small digital recorder. "I have pages of ideas in a notebook. Every time something comes to me I add to it." Her digital recorder holds 200 songs, but after a song is demoed, Robbins erases the work track to make more room. She has notebooks dating back to 1986. "The good thing about using a notebook is you can go back and look at the work pages," she explains. She is also adept at writing to tracks, especially in pop and dance music. "I can close my eyes and just completely sing whatever comes out of my mouth and record 10 ideas, then go back and find a verse, pre-chorus, and chorus that I like. It's not a thinking process."

She is an increasingly rare breed: a successful songwriter who is not a producer, whose strength is her uncanny ability to write songs under virtually any circumstances in a wide scope of styles. Still, everyday, Lindy Robbins is on the line. "There are plenty of days

I'm driving to a writing session and I'm thinking, 'I want to go to the mall, I want to go to the movies, I want to go to the beach, I want my mommy,' but you have to force yourself to work hard."

Luis Resto: Lost in the Music

It was Luis Resto, resplendent in his Detroit Piston jersey, who stepped up to accept the award when Barbra Streisand announced "Lose Yourself" from *8 Mile*, recorded by Eminem, as Song of the Year at the 75th Annual Academy Awards. Resto is a Detroit native in his forties who has worked with artists from Anita Baker to Patti Smith to Was (Not Was). Now, in collaboration with Marshall Mathers (Eminem) and Jeff Bass, he's an improbable, elated Oscar winner.

"I started piano at nine," Resto recalls. "My brother Mario was my biggest influence since he was a guitarist and songwriter." Resto's parents were always supportive of their boys' musical endeavors; his father even took them to see Jimi Hendrix at Cobo Arena in 1968 when Luis was still in elementary school. "I remember leaving the parking lot. This guy came around checking everyone's car horn tones and we all honked the intro to "Purple Haze," he laughs.

Fusion music, John McLaughlin, Jan Hammer, and Herbie Hancock mesmerized the young Resto, but he needed a synthesizer. "I said to my dad, 'It's so expensive, but there's something in that.'" At 12 and a half years of age, he began playing an ARP Odyssey. Then, at a police auction, a Fender Rhodes, bass amp, and Electro-Voice mic came into his possession for $101. "That's what began my stay in my brother Mario's group," Resto relates.

Don Was remembers his first encounter with Resto. "When he was 15 he was my friend's piano student. My friend called me up and said, 'You've to hear this guy and use him on a record.'" Resto reflects, "I think I appreciate Was (Not Was) more now. At the time I was a pain in the ass. But with Was there were no boundaries." In the mid-'90s, Resto spent seven months in Los Angeles playing on Was' productions and pondering a move to the West coast until he received an offer to return home to play with Patti Smith. "Patti was this figure for me," Resto offers. "My brother brought home Patti Smith's *Horses* when I was 12 or 13. I'd listen over and over and stare at that cover. Then, 20 years later, to have this opportunity was a highlight."

It was Resto's longtime colleague, Joel Martin, who connected Resto with Marshall Mathers. He worked on both *The Eminem Show* and *8 Mile*, collaborating on songs and score for the latter. Additionally, he has worked with 50 Cent and Shady Records' signees. Most significantly, Resto is acknowledged as a co-writer, a fact that bears enormous economic implications as Mathers, who could certainly play it any way he chooses, takes the high road. "I know the other side very well," Resto muses. "I don't say it in a bad way. That's what I grew up accustomed to. Here's this grand payoff. Who would have thought? You don't get these kind of record sales, and for Marshall to give it up as such is remarkable."

Work with Mathers is full out. "That's what he does. He's concerned with (daughter) Halie, and that's his main occupation, getting the next beat out of his head and getting the next project for the artists on his label." Sessions begin around 2:00 P.M. "I'll walk in and he'll be at the drum machine tapping on something, and then I boot up my keyboards and some melody strikes him, and that's a good sign. That can evolve to anything in the next half hour because he's busy adding to that beat. Where it started from might be completely different from where it ends up. We always have a DAT going, catching everything that's happening."

And this is the collaboration that brought Resto to the stage of the Kodak Theater, and to accepting the award from Streisand. "I've done every gig in the book: weddings, solo gigs, Knights of Columbus halls. When I saw her, all I could think of were those daddy/daughter dances to 'The Way We Were' and 'Evergreen.' I thought, 'Oh my God, it's the artist whose music I used to play at weddings!' And that's pretty classic."

Bob Malone: Road Warrior

Everything about Bob Malone—from his stride-influenced piano chops to his gravelly Dixie growl—seems like a compass pointing toward the Crescent City. But sounds are deceiving; Malone is actually from New Jersey. He's spent a number of years in Los Angeles, and he has lived for extended periods in New York and, yes, New Orleans, too.

"New York and New Orleans are the only cities where they have pianos in every club," Malone intones. "In New York because no one wants to carry any gear, and in New Orleans because there are so many piano players."

This seasoned road warrior has toured with The Neville Brothers, opened for the Rev. Al Green and Manhattan Transfer, and performed at countless festivals ,including Kerrville and Falcon Ridge. It shows: Malone is an electrifying live performer, having learned how to drop the proverbial hammer by opening shows. "They don't want to hear the opening act," he explains. "But you can win them over."

Most often he traverses a cross-continental road, performing 150 dates a year as a headlining artist in concert venues that seat anywhere from 50 to 500 patrons. "Doing those rooms is my biggest impetus to tour," he states. Malone's two Delta Moon/Chartmaker releases, *The Darkest Part of the Night* and *Bob Malone*, combined with his relentless touring schedule, have earned this tenacious troubadour a national audience and an enviable sheaf of kudos.

Given his impressive sales figures and touring visibility, it would seem that signing with a major label could take him up to the next level. "I've come very close a lot of times," he confesses. "I don't know if this will change with the new record, but I've had a problem with classification. They're not sure what it is or what to do with it. That's the reason I've been independent; it's not by choice."

Independence is not for the lazy. Malone books his shows, handles the promo, sets up the interviews, and drives the van. He even chronicles his road adventures in vivid prose on his Web site (www.bobmalone.com), and he's contributing to a new book, *Working Musicians*, due this fall from Harper Collins.

Selling CDs on the road accounts for half of Malone's income. "When I first started touring, a lot of the gigs didn't pay. I was opening for acts in cool rooms where I got seen, and I'd put on a good enough show that everyone would buy my record. I'd go into some freebie gig and make $300 in sales. I lived off of that. It was the last step of turning me into a strong live act. Desperation is a wonderful motivator."

Prior to the road gigs, Malone admits he spent time sitting around in L.A. awaiting a magic record deal. "I was doing top-40 gigs, shit I hated. I finally said 'I'm not going to do this.' You can't be taken seriously as an artist and then go play cover tunes six nights a week. They can smell it on you. Audiences *know*; you have to be that guy, the artist. It all changed for me when I decided not to do that anymore—[then] I was taken seriously."

Summary

These four artists epitomize one crucial career key: They never got out of the business; instead, they discovered viable avenues to project themselves and their music. They also epitomize a sterling networking strategy: Only those who are left standing will succeed.

CHAPTER 10

Go Where You Wanna Go

Leaving the security of your home and moving to another location can be a daunting reality, but it may well be necessary for the advancement of your career. This chapter evaluates the scenes in the major U.S. music capitals.

In one six-year span in my first music business incarnation as a songwriter, musician, and performer, I lived in, and survived, all three music capitals. Today, as an author and a journalist, I make my home in Los Angeles, but I am in daily contact with New York and Nashville, where I travel for interviews and other projects. Eventually, if you aspire to a professional music career, you too will need to correspond with, pitch to, visit, write, record, or live in one (if not all three) of these dynamic cities. If your aspirations guide you, you too must search for the ideal locale for your talents and be willing to pack up your tent and move to more verdant pastures, to go where it is, or to make it happen where you are.

Nashville

Nashville's reverence for the song form cannot be overstated. These days, it's not just country in Music City either. Christian, pop, rock, gospel, alternative—and especially alt.country and Americana—are also viable forms. Nashville is a city of surprises; the rumpled-looking gentleman sitting next to you at a coffee shop could be a major songwriter, executive, or record producer. Certain parts of town near Music Row are similar to a college campus in which many of the patrons in the restaurants are in the music business. Nashville respects longevity and credibility, and personal relationships are key in this friendly, song-oriented town. Most of the major music publishers have offices, and many smaller boutique companies exist, too. If you plan to visit, you will need to research publishers and contact them regarding their submission policies and the possibility of setting up appointments.

IF YOU VISIT

The songwriting business is localized, stretching along Music Row (16th and 17th Avenues) in refurbished homes and newer office suites. Hotel rooms cost from $50 to $200 per night; budget motels tend to be in the outlying parts of town. If you're planning on sightseeing, you'll probably need a car.

Nashville Songwriters Association International (NSAI) is a valuable resource. If you can, schedule your trip in the spring when NSAI produces their annual event, Tin Pan South, with a slate of hit songwriter concerts, showcases, open mics, classes, panels, and workshops. Another new NSAI program, Songwriters Symposium, is a two-day fall event that offers pitch sessions and evaluations from some of Music City's most esteemed publishers and record company executives.

The Songwriters Guild of America (SGA) is another strongly supportive organization with a slate of song critiques and ASK-A-PRO sessions to connect and educate writers. You have to be a member to take advantage of their events. You can reach them at 615-329-1782 or online at www.songwriters.org.

Other events in town include the Nashville New Music Conference, also held in mid-fall, which is a four-day event with major industry participation. Highlights include a trade show, technology forum, panel discussions, mentor sessions, keynote speakers, and a studio tour of Nashville. Information is at www.2nmc.com. The Americana Music Association Conference, held in the fall, features over 600 industry professionals in an array of panels, discussions, and performances all specific to the Americana format. Information is at www.americanamusic.org.

The Songwriter and Musician's Guide to Nashville, authored by Sherry Bond (Allworth Press), is an invaluable resource for the visiting songwriter.

SHOWCASES AND OPEN MICS

There are a variety of places to perform, including the very famous Bluebird Cafe. *Nashville Scene,* published every Wednesday and free at bookstores and coffee shops, has comprehensive listings of clubs. There are Writers' Nights going on every night of the week, including open mic events where you can line up and sign up to play that evening. Most, however, are planned. Some hosts are flexible, so if you have a persuasive personality, or if there has been a cancellation, you might get a chance to perform that night. If you're going to be in town for a few days, check out your chosen club early in your stay, and see if you can be scheduled to perform later in your visit. Your set may consist of only two to four songs and should be original (not cover) tunes.

The BMI Music Connection Showcase series is held at various venues in Nashville and features today's hit songwriters as well as up-and-comers. It's free and open to the public. The BMI Acoustic Roundup, held the second Thursday of every month at the Sutler, pairs the top names in songwriting with soon-to-break through talent. The BMI RoundTable was created in order to arm songwriters with powerful information that will help them navigate today's highly competitive music industry. RoundTable topics include performing rights, BMI's history, how the Nashville music industry operates, and tips to help you become the songwriter you want to be. It is held the second Monday of each month at the BMI Nashville offices and is open to all songwriters. For more information, contact the BMI Writer/Publisher Relations Department at 615-401-2000. The BMI Songwriters Workshop with Jason Blume is generally held the second Tuesday of each month from and invites all songwriters who are serious about and committed to successful commercial songwriting to attend. At each workshop, Jason Blume examines the components of hit songs and covers a variety of topics, including song structure, lyric and melody writing techniques, musical hooks, writing from the heart for the radio, and effective demo recording, among others. There is no cost to attend, but seating is limited, so advance registration is required.

IF YOU DECIDE TO MOVE THERE

Nashville has a temperate climate, housing is moderately priced, and the countryside is stunning. Keep in mind that although the music industry is free thinking, you are in the South—a locale that is historically not as progressive as the Nashville arts and entertainment communities would indicate.

NINE STEPS TO NASHVILLE

1. Don't expect to open all of the doors overnight. Nashville is a town that respects history, longevity, and credibility.

2. Take enough money to at least give the illusion of some level of success. If at all possible, stay with friends. If you're planning on sightseeing, you'll probably need a car.

3. The business people here are incredibly savvy. Don't assume that you're dealing with yokels. Nashville doesn't care what you've done elsewhere.

4. Use your performing rights organization to help you open doors. Contact them well in advance of your visit, but don't expect them to perform miracles on your behalf.

5. Nashville Songwriters Association International (NSAI) is a valuable resource—especially if you're a member. For membership information, contact them at (800) 321-6008 or (615) 256-3354 and check out their Web site at www.Nashvillesongwriters.com. All members receive a booklet when joining that features a variety of information, including hotel listings and other information to maximize a visit to Nashville.

6. There are people in Nashville who will rip you off by asking you to pay them up to $5,000 to get you a deal. Even if it's all in the name of production costs, you can be taken for a ride. Yes, you may wind up with a CD, but it won't be on a major label, and you may have paid four times too much to record it. Always be wary of name-droppers and people who make promises with price tags attached.

7. *Music Row*, a trade publication, is an excellent source for an insider's look at the Nashville music scene. Learn the names and positions of the movers and shakers.

8. With demos, the simpler the better. Since Nashville is a song town, your demo doesn't have to be as highly polished. A guitar/vocal or piano/vocal is often sufficient.

9. Nashville takes the music industry very seriously, and the caliber of talent is in the stratosphere. There's a lot of pride in this quality; don't ever sell that short. The only people who wear cowboy hats and boots in Nashville are tourists.

New York

From Tin Pan Alley to the Brill Building, from Broadway to Greenwich Village, music is the soundtrack to successive eras of history in the Big Apple. Since New York is the center of the theater world, there are many outlets and opportunities for songwriters and composers who create for the stage and cabaret. The pop world is well represented, too, as are hip-hop and R&B, with the current climate heavily favoring songwriter/producers. Most major music publishers are in midtown Manhattan, but the center of the songwriting world is Greenwich Village, with its cafés, coffeehouses, and clubs presenting a wide spectrum of acoustic and songwriter-oriented shows.

DOWNTOWN

The New York Songwriters' Circle is a showcase held twice monthly at The Bitter End (147 Bleecker Street in The Village) that features many of the city's most distinguished songsmiths alongside up-and-coming singer/songwriters. Artists are selected via word of mouth or from tapes heard in listening sessions. They now book up to eight months in advance. You can find information at www.songwriters-circle.com.

UMO Music presents a Sunday showcase at the Baggot Inn (82 W. 3RD Street between Sullivan Street and Thompson Street) most Sundays in the winter but only if the weather is bad in the summer. Sign-up is at the door. Information is at www.umo.com. The Cornelia Street Café (9 Cornelia Street, 212-989-9319) presents The Songwriters Beat, a monthly showcase of original songwriters. Booking information is at www. corneliastreetcafe.com or www.songwritersbeat.com. SESAC's Writers on the Storm, currently in residence at The Cutting Room, features four of the organization's writers in a showcase format. Due to the success of club alumni Norah Jones, The Living Room, also in the Village, is home to a major scene.

ASCAP Writers at Night is an intimate showcase series designed to feature the talents of promising new songwriters, while providing them with an opportunity to forge new relationships in a laid-back and supportive atmosphere. It's currently held every first Tuesday of the month.

SONGS ABOVE THE FOOTLIGHTS

ASCAP and the Manhattan Association of Cabarets (MAC) have instigated a showcase program where cabaret and theater songwriters present new material before an audience of publishers and other songwriters. The ASCAP Foundation also presents a showcase series, Thru The Walls, that spotlights concert-trained composer/performers who cross genres. Contact the Society at wwwmacnyc.com.

BMI and the late Lehman Engel joined forces to create a setting where new writers for the musical theatre could learn their craft. The BMI Lehman Engel Musical Theatre Workshop continues to flourish and is considered to be the foremost training ground for new writing voices, bringing forth musical milestones such as *A Chorus Line, Little Shop of Horrors, Nine,* and *Ragtime.* The Workshop presents a series of in-house cabarets that attract music and theatrical industry attention. The Workshop participates both formally and informally with various New York and regional theaters in developmental programs. Contact BMI at 212-830-2508 or via e-mail at theatreworkshop@bmi.com.

SONGWRITERS HALL OF FAME

The Songwriters Hall of Fame and the National Academy of Popular Music sponsor meetings where music industry professionals enlighten and educate attendees on both the craft and the business aspects of songwriting. These are held eight times per year, followed by open mics co-hosted by Bob Leone and April Anderson. For more information, contact Bob Leone at 212-957-9230 or via e-mail at info@songwritershalloffame.org. Current members of the National Academy of Popular Music (NAPM) are also eligible to submit songs for Songwriters

Hall of Fame Songwriter Showcases, which are held four times annually. You'll need to submit materials at least two months in advance of the shows.

IF YOU VISIT

Manhattan is where you'll want to be, and it's not cheap. Check out a Web travel service like Expedia.com or Travelocity.com for the best deals. Hotels shouldn't be your priority, since in this dynamic "city that never sleeps" (to paraphrase Kander and Ebb) you'll find many things to occupy your time entertainment- and business-wise. The city itself is a breeze to navigate via taxis or well-designated busses and subways, taking you anywhere you need to go. It's inspiring to walk, too. Just remember that numbered streets descend as you head downtown and you can't get lost. Pick up a copy of the venerable *Village Voice* for all of the club listings.

IF YOU DECIDE TO MOVE THERE

New York rents are among the most astronomical in the country. Some musicians opt to live in Brooklyn or Queens, which are cheaper, or across the river in New Jersey. The trains can whisk you anywhere quickly. For acoustic artists, there is a distinct advantage in living in New York because it is a hub of activity with close proximity to other Northeast towns (especially Boston) that have strong performing scenes and a multitude of venues for singer/songwriters.

Los Angeles

Los Angeles is a package town. Songwriters and artists succeed because they are somehow connected—to artists, producers, films, and other media. In this ever mutating city of the angels (or perhaps more appropriately, the "city of the angles"), the song is an essential component. Writer/producer teams of two or three specialists—e.g., a producer, a groove maestro, and a lyricist—are highly valued, while the era of the single, unconnected song (if it ever existed) has been supplanted by a corporate, high-stakes publishing environment.

FILM AND TELEVISION

The explosion of film, network and cable television, and video games has spawned innumerable outlets for new music and songs. Songs that mirror what's happening on the charts (as of this writing, edgy alternative rock and singer/songwriters) are the most requested and easily placed. Check out www.filmmusicworld.com.

The Songwriters Guild of America (SGA) produces a variety of educational events, including their ASK-A-PRO series. SGA membership is available to all, and the Hollywood office is an unfailingly writer-friendly environment. There are always ongoing classes as well. Contact SGA at 323-462-1108 or online at www.songwriters.org.

Another local songwriting group produces well-regarded activities, including ongoing songwriter showcases and educational events. As their Web site says, "The L.A. Songwriters' Network (www.songnet.org) seeks to establish, develop, promote, and sustain for the songwriting community in Los Angeles, and for the global songwriting virtual 'cyber-community', free and low-cost access to the tools required to improve their craft, build successful careers, host and promote workshops and events, and most importantly give back to the world better music, better lyrics, greater positive, wholesome, uplifting, sincere, and genuine musical and artistic creation and expression."

PERFORMING RIGHTS

If you belong to ASCAP, try to plan your songwriting trip around the General Member Meeting, now held in L.A. every other year in early February. Year round, ASCAP hosts educational events, including Music Business 101 and The Songwriters Studio, plus their highly regarded acoustic showcase, Quiet on the Set. This show has spawned a spin-off, the Cover Me series, which celebrates writers whose works have been covered by prominent artists. Past participants have included Vonda Shepard, Jill Sobule, Willie Nile, Joseph Arthur, Sixpence None the Richer, Jonatha Brooke, Ben Harper, Catie Curtis, Allen Shamblin, Deana Carter, Rufus Wainwright, and John Mayer.

BMI's contributions to Los Angeles' night life and their continued high-octane shows—BMI's Circle of Songs, Songwriters Club, and Pick of the Month among them—are some of the showcase tickets in town. Information is available at BMI's Web site, www.bmi.com, or www.circleofsongs.com. SESAC now has a West coast office located in Santa Monica and has begun presenting highly regarded industry showcases and educational events for their members.

GET CONNECTED

For the past 27 years, *Music Connection* magazine has measured the pulse of L.A.'s music business. *Music Connection* publishes special editions throughout the year, including a guide to music publishers, music supervisors, open mics, and showcases. The "Song Biz" column, my domain, has information about performing rights organizations, publishing companies, and show-cases. You can read the current issue online at www.musicconnection.com or call 818-955-0101 for subscription information.

The distances in Los Angeles are vast. The music community is spread from the beach towns of Santa Monica and Venice inland to West Hollywood, Hollywood central, Silverlake, and the San Fernando Valley, especially Universal City, Studio City, and North Hollywood. For acoustic performers, *Li'l Hal's Guide* (www.halsguide.com) is the definitive resource for locating open mic and showcase clubs. Taxi, the independent A&R service, holds their annual convention, the Road Rally, in the fall. It's a weekend of classes, panels, pitch sessions, etc. You have to be a member to attend, but the event itself is free. Check out www.taxi.com. There are other events in the early stages of development, including a Songsalive! Expo for independent artists (www.songsalive.org), and Loyola Marymount Law School and California Lawyers for the Arts present an industry panel in the fall that is an excellent networking resource. Lastly, UCLA Extension's Music Business programs present one free day of songwriter events every September to promote their upcoming classes.

IF YOU DECIDE TO MOVE THERE

Los Angeles may remind you of the fable of the blind men and the elephant because every part of it you touch feels different. You can live in a roaring city, in the tranquil suburbs, at the beach, in a small town, high in the hills in a neighborhood of palatial mansions, or deep inside the barrio and still be within the city limits.

Emerging Cities

With a population of 425,000, Atlanta is only the thirty-ninth largest city in the United States, but there is a supportive network of musicians, clubs, radio, and publications in the city that help set it apart.

For R&B artists and songwriters, Atlanta, Georgia, has become the musical capital of the New South. Ludacris, OutKast, and P. Diddy have homes there, and it's not only home to soul music—The Black Crowes, Collective Soul, Indigo Girls, Shawn Mullins, Elton John, and John Mayer base their operations there as well.

One of the things that has made it easier for bands to emerge, and possible for them to survive, is the abundance of local clubs that feature live music in East Atlanta, Little Five Points, and Midtown.

When it comes to hip-hop, Atlanta is unrivaled. Rappers and artists who may have started in the Big Apple or in the City of Angels have migrated to Atlanta. Another extension of the Atlanta music scene is underground dance clubs and DJs, and another supportive outlet that helps Atlanta's music scene thrive is local radio. Both Album 88 (WRAS-FM 88.5), GA State University's student-run station, and 99X (WNNX-FM 99.7), the city's "alternative" station, have given local bands the chance to be heard. Album 88 does it with the Georgia Music show, and 99X gives bands airtime on "Local Only," which can be heard via the station's Internet site, 99X.com, and sponsors the Locals-Only Stage, during Atlanta's annual Music Midtown Festival.

All Over the Map

If you are a visiting musician, songwriter, or aspiring executive, your success will be determined by your interaction with the people you meet. It is imperative to do your homework before visiting any of these locales, to make a strong, enduring impression once you're there, and to follow up and keep in touch with your contacts when you leave. ASCAP, BMI, or SESAC members should make a visit to their performing rights organization a first stop, but be realistic: Don't expect them to perform miracles on your behalf.

Music Conferences

Maybe you're not prepared to make the move yet to a major recording capital, but when you do, you'll need contacts. Music conferences proliferate in all genres of music. A dedicated Web search will display events coast to coast. These are invaluable opportunities to make lasting contacts, and the information and contacts to be gained by attending a songwriting conference cannot be over-emphasized. It's more than just a place to meet—it's empowerment, a sense of community, the joy of belonging. Many participants share that they come away significantly inspired by these experiences.

Of all the annual events, two come to mind quickly. The Durango Song Expo (www.durangosong.com), as its name would indicate, was first held in Durango, Colorado. The locale has now shifted to Telluride, and the same organization is producing a songwriting event in the wine country just north of Santa Barbara. Imagine the combination of hundreds of songwriters and endless bottles of great wine!

The Durango folks pride themselves on limiting the number of registrants so that everyone will have an opportunity to have their songs heard by industry reps from Nashville and Los Angeles. The pros and the writers tend to be slanted toward country/roots/Americana, so if you create in these fields, you're in luck. Panels cover everything from copyright basics to promotion and publicity with hit songwriter concerts and long nights of guitar pulls in many of the rooms.

The second of these events is the West Coast Songwriters Conference (www.westcoastsongwriter.org). With 16 seminars, 50 song screening sessions, 1,500 songs reviewed, performance showcases, one-on-one sessions, and concerts, the conference is a wellspring of opportunities for over 500 songwriter/musicians who attend the event.

It's just close enough to Los Angeles to draw a strong cross-section of Hollywood publishers and record label execs. The vibe of the conference is endlessly supportive; there's a respect for the songwriter that goes far beyond monetary commercialization, and many types of music are represented.

15 Tips to Maximize Your Conference Experience

1. Bigger is not necessarily better. Some of the smaller regional conferences can be more valuable than a huge, confusing cattle call.

2. Plan, plan, plan. You can generally save big bucks by registering early.

3. Minimize lodging costs by sharing rooms or staying with friends.

4. Don't assume that if you're staying at a hotel where the conference is held you'll pay less with a group rate. Check out the possibilities online; sometimes you're better off booking a room on your own.

5. If you stay in a hotel where the event is held, specify if you'll be in a "quiet" area. At the Folk Alliance Conferences it's not unusual for musicians to jam all night. Consequently, a quiet wing of the hotel is reserved for those who require some sleeping silence.

6. Do research. Anticipate what classes, panels, and workshops you want to attend. Often these are the most valuable events happening.

7. Again, the purpose is to open doors and windows. Pressing press kits and CDs into everyone's hands can be off-putting. I often leave conventions overwhelmed. What I appreciate is someone asking for my card and contacting me in the next week when I'm not deluged.

8. Mixers and social events are a key component of conferences and conventions. Save your energy for late-night schmoozing.

9. When you return home, don't procrastinate: File all of the names and contacts you made.

10. Write thank you letters to panel participants whose presentations you particularly enjoyed.

11. Your most valuable contacts will probably be the other attendees.

12. Dress comfortably but distinctively. Project a vibe.

13. If possible, set up meetings in advance of the event. Proffering an invitation for a meal (you pay!) is a generous way to interact.

14. The booth areas are also valuable places to meet people in a natural setting, especially at slow times or lunch hours.

15. See if you can volunteer to assist at the event. Some conferences will comp volunteers.

World Beat

As I teach students from the U.K., Norway, Germany, Japan, the Philippines, and the U.S., I emphasize that pop music is a global phenomenon. Sometimes what is successful in one part of the world spreads across the continents; other times, the payoff is more localized. As music industry professionals, we need to be apprised of the explosive potential of world markets.

There are many examples of U.S. artists who first became successful in the U.K. A struggling sideman for Little Richard, Jimi Hendrix came to prominence in the U.K. before returning to conquer the states at the Monterey Pop Festival.

In the following decade, an aspiring rock singer from Ohio, Chrissy Hynde, moved from Akron to London to form The Pretenders, who were similarly successful stateside only after their breakthrough in Britain. The lowly Ramones, jokes in their hometown, blew away English audiences and inspired a whole generation of punks before returning in leather-jacketed triumph to their native New York.

The market for songs is worldwide, too. Los Angeles songwriter Michéle Vice-Maslin has made a living for years writing songs for global markets: in the U.K., Denmark, Spain, Scandinavia, Belgium, and Holland. What's her secret? "I pitch through [the U.K. magazine] *SongLink*," she says. "I've gone to MIDEM six times. I went to the Music Bridges trip to Ireland and the D'Pop writers week in Denmark. I know all of the A&R people all over the world, and I solicit them. When I was signed to publishing deals, I would find out who the local publishers were in each country, and I'd call them and send them my songs. Also, I'd buy international music trades and really research them."

This proactivity leads to contacts. As Vice-Maslin says, it was her personal relationships with music business people worldwide that sustained her until her first huge U.S. hit, in a songwriting career that has spanned 20-plus years.

Further Afield

London—a pop, dance, and techno music center—is a co-writer's Mecca, since much of the pop recording is project oriented. Liverpool and Manchester also have vibrant music scenes. Stockholm, Sweden, has emerged as a pop capital in the past decade. And don't rule out Tokyo, Japan, or Seoul, South Korea. And with China becoming a major world power, it's only a matter of time before there's bling-bling in Beijing.

Begin your global music education by reading the trades (*Billboard* has a listing of world charts) and check out Vice-Maslin's recommended publication, *SongLink,* for a listing of acts worldwide who need material. You can also search the Internet for many variations on this theme.

The business of music is different for each city, state, and country. However, the real tools—contacts, people skills, persistence, and dedication—are absolutely identical, no matter what market you're in.

CHAPTER 11

Defining Your Direction

By now, you've hopefully absorbed enough positive information to help you make real choices in your career. But if you've been banging your head against the wall, trying to make things happen, perhaps it's time for an inner dialogue with yourself.

It is all too easy to ignore things that don't exist. Writing down your goals, your ambitions, your hopes and dreams should be the very first step in planning your year.

I spend the last week in December devising a list of what I want to happen in the upcoming year, whether it's a new position, a show I'd like to produce, artists I want to interview, or a book I want to write. Twelve months later, I'm always amazed to see that although all the new benchmarks I'd set for myself may not have been reached, many others have. And it's because of my efforts on behalf of my primary goals that the secondary events occurred. Motion begets motion.

You can stir up the universe by transmitting and expending your energy correctly. I know this may sound like some California New-Age malarkey, but try focusing and devoting your energy to achieving your goals. Weekly, daily, and monthly "to-do" lists are effective ways to track your progress. Remember, all of those small things you accomplish will eventually add up.

The following questions are for you to answer only to yourself.

Questions for Artists

1. *How important is your career to your life?*
   Successful music business practitioners do not go from one comfortable situation to another. Would you be willing to move to another city? To go on the road? To leave friends and family behind in the pursuit of your dreams?

2. *Can you make it happen where you are?*
   As discussed earlier in this book, the music business now has other centers of creativity. Creating a scene in your hometown, with similar bands, media, and artists, can help you attract attention to your music. But it takes a willingness to be proactive and to work tirelessly and a certain personality to convince others that they should work for the good of all.

3. *Do you have reference points for your music?*
   If so, is it in a style that is viable for new audiences? Remember, buyers for music are progressively younger.

4. *Are you performing regionally?*
   It's imperative to expand audiences for live music. It may even cost you to travel to another area to perform, but in the long run it will be well worth the investment.

5. *Are you making too much money working a straight job?*
   At some point you'll need to define yourself strictly as a music professional—sink or swim time. It's difficult to devote eight hours a day to working for someone else and then attempt to do music full time. You may need to cut your job loose—usually a harrowing, but often necessary, proposition.

6. *Are you improving your chops?*
   Classes, workshops, and lessons are not only essential to pursuing your art, but also to making new contacts.

7. *Are your aspirations viable?*
   Dreams are marvelous, but you have to live in the moment as well. The great thing about outreach, personal contacts, and networking strategies is that you can practice them every single day of your life.

8. *Do others like working with you?*
   Even the most talented musician won't get work if no one likes being around him. In Los Angeles, for example, where the talent pool is phenomenal, it goes far beyond technique when it comes time to call up players for high-paying sessions. It's more about vibe—that the best musicians also bring in enthusiasm, a "can-do" attitude, and make everyone feel like they're on a winning team.

9. *Do you have a vibe?*
   This is an intangible quality, but it's an energy, an aura, something that makes others respond to you—the

elusive "star quality." I can detect it, but I can't explain it; still, if you aspire to a career as a major recording artist, others will need to feel it coming off of you.

10. *Do you fear success?*
There are many ways to sabotage your own intentions, either consciously or unconsciously. Using alcohol or drugs, overeating, or taking health risks are the most obvious. But do you alienate others, forget to return telephone calls, or in general not take care of business? If so, you may not feel you deserve to be successful.

I am not a psychologist or a psychiatrist (at least not a trained or accredited one!), but I know that it's much harder to be successful than to not be. Success will lose you many more friends than failure. More will be expected, others will resent and be intimidated by you, and it may be difficult to decide whether people like you or your position. Talent is not its own reward. The perils of instant fortune are well known.

Questions for Aspiring Moguls

1. *Do you read the trades every week?*
If so, do you know the names of the movers and shakers in the music business, and can you track their movements? Do you study their pictures to be able to recognize them on sight if necessary?

2. *Have you relocated to a music center?*
As discussed many times in this book, you either have to create it where you are or go to where it is.

3. *Do you recognize talent in others?*
   Try predicting which movies will do well, what singers will be selected on *American Idol* and shows of this ilk. Are you usually correct?

4. *Can you champion, and sell, artists?*
   Make no mistake: it's all sales. Being able to convince others and to transmit enthusiasm and emotion is a major attribute of music industry professionals.

5. *Do you present yourself correctly?*
   Music people can recognize others. It's a hip, fast-moving world. A strait-laced suit-wearing businessman may alienate musicians. Even if you're on the other side of the desk, you're expected to have a "look."

6. *Do you have a handle on economics?*
   Planning, strategizing, and tracking income and expenses are valuable abilities for anyone hoping to handle and earn large sums of money.

7. *Can you go with the flow?*
   Virtually every situation in the music business happens at the last possible second. Being overly rigid therefore can be detrimental in an environment where plans are always changing. Musicians typically follow their own clocks, and working with them requires an understanding of creative chronology.

8. *Do you see the big picture?*
   Artist managers and other handlers of talent must be able to deal with the details at hand but also must be able to visualize what will occur much further down the road. This requires a master plan. Are you capable of such a long-term commitment to others?

9. *Do you have the time to devote to my career?*
It is virtually impossible to launch viable enterprises if you don't have the time or energy to do so. You cannot buy your way into this business; it's insular, and relationships run long and deep.

10. *Are you enterprising enough to create your own niche market?*
The music business utilizes everything from voice and performance coaches to dentists who specialize in trumpet players' teeth. Possibly you have a skill that could be tailored to the music business. Remember:There are no rules; only your own creativity is devising outlets and applications for you talents.

Teamwork

Other than the film business, the music business is probably the most interactive enterprise in the entertainment industry. Artists are the visible tip of the iceberg, supported by an immense cast of players who may be less evident but are none the less equally vital and, in most cases, will probably enjoy longer careers than the artist. This section examines some of the principal players from two sides: one, if you're an artist needing to engage team members, and two, necessary qualifications if you want to work in any of these essential fields.

Management

"I need to find an agent or a manager," you say. But which do you need? The duties, responsibilities, and qualifications are totally different. First, there are managers. Back in the day, managers were often solo operators—savvy visionaries who would attach themselves to artists and guide each and every aspect of the artist's career. Long-term relationships were the norm: Brian Epstein with the Beatles, Colonel Tom Parker with Elvis, and Albert Grossman with Bob Dylan. (Interestingly enough, Grossman never used the term "manager." He preferred the more general "works with the artist" to describe his duties.)

A manager is many things: counselor, sounding board, partner, Svengali—depending, of course, on the needs of the artist. Above all, he or she is an employee—hired by the artist to oversee all elements.

When Do You Need a Manager?

This is easy: when you can no longer run your own business affairs because you've become too successful. When artists tell me they think they need a manager, my first question is always, "How much income are you currently generating?" If the answer is none, nil, nada, the correct response is "Why do you need a manager?"

I've done everything within the management sphere: hand holding, brow beating, booking dates, hauling gear, and bailing my clients out of jail. The question of what a manager does is answered by the phrase, "Whatever is necessary." I would always give keys to my house to artists I managed in case they needed a safe haven, peace and quiet, or a place to do their laundry.

Handling clients signed to record deals is a taxing existence. I discovered I was spending more time with the label than with the artists. And I learned that if events, projects, and tours went well, it was always because of the artist. If things fell flat or were less than successful, it was always because of management. A manager has to take the blows for the artist.

What to Look For in a Manager

So if a manager is interested in you or your act, is it best to sign with the biggest one? Not necessarily. I've known new artists signed to high-profile managers who have fared poorly because the manager's attention was invariably focused on his bigger, higher-earning clients, not the ones who were still struggling to find an audience.

Technically, anyone can call himself a manager without having any qualifications whatsoever, and that's a dicey proposition for most new artists. It is better to have no manager than to have the wrong one, because he or she will inevitably alienate those whom you need to cultivate.

Record labels will rarely sign artists without proper management in place. Sometimes if an A&R executive is interested in signing an act without management, he will recommend someone he knows. This can be an excellent way to come in from a position of power. Beware the manager who comes in simply to sign you to a label, however. It is not unknown for unscrupulous A&R execs to be in cahoots with managers to skim and split a percentage of the signing bonus offered by a record label. That has happened.

A good manager is with you for the long term, is sympathetic to the artist, can see the big picture, and can facilitate a wide range of scenarios, from negotiating record deals and sync licenses to publishing and touring. A great manager doesn't need to know everything, but he has to know how to find out everything. And he takes 15% to 20% of your earnings in exchange for this expertise.

Do You Want to Be a Manager?

Managers are a special breed in the business. If you are organized, understand how the business works, and are well connected, aggressive, and irrepressible, you have some necessary attributes. Some managers are hard-driving street hustlers, some are smooth Ivy League law school graduates—but all are capable of multitasking, and not only recognizing talent but knowing how to make the most of it. A good manager says "yes" to virtually any situation and then figures out how to make the most of it.

Your Lawyer

Lawyers in the music business are different than lawyers in the civilian world. They are paid hourly or on a retainer basis. Few reputable lawyers in Los Angeles will shop packages to labels. Beware of an up-front fee from those who do so.

Donald S. Passman, author of *All You Need to Know About the Music Business,* is a high-profile Hollywood music business attorney whose reputation is irreproachable. Jay Cooper is another high-stakes player, as is Peter Paterno. But we're talking major billings for their services, probably in excess of $600 an hour. Unless you're negotiating a multi-million dollar agreement, it's doubtful you need someone on this level.

On the other end of the spectrum is a cadre of eager young lawyers fresh out of law school and eager to earn a reputation in the high-stakes music world who charge a fraction of these fees. Often these lawyers are out in the clubs, discovering talent, the same as any other operative in the music business.

Having a lawyer with whom the label is familiar may be to your advantage, but keep in mind that some major labels will hire lawyers to work for them simply to keep them in the pocket when it comes time to negotiation deals with artists—a distinct disadvantage and a clear conflict of interest. But a good lawyer is necessary when it's time to sign contracts. And I've seen sympathetic lawyers defer billing altogether if they have a relationship with an artist who is having money problems.

Agents

Agents work for the buyer, period. Yes, you'll need an agent if you are successful, have a major deal, and are ready to tour; otherwise, you may be better off booking yourself. Agents are extremely selective and generally sign only artists who they know they can work in specific markets; rarely will they take a chance on an unknown.

As with other elements, it's all about relationships: in this case, between the agent and the buyer. In the state of

California, an agent posts a bond with the state in order to be licensed and qualified. As a holdover from the dark days of the movie business, it's not possible for someone to be both an agent and a manager—this is considered a conflict of interest.

Agents generally earn 10% to 15% of their artists' gross earnings from performances, and they deduct expenses incurred as well. The agent takes his clues from the manager, finds out what fees are necessary, how far the artist will travel, audience specifics, packaging, plans for recording and touring, special needs, plus sound and lighting.

The most effective agents are highly specialized, dealing in a specific genre of music—Latin, jazz, world, or rock, for example. If you have the qualifications to be an agent, you're probably already doing it: booking bands at shows or parties.

Your Publicist

You need a publicist only if you have a story to tell and a product to sell. Nothing could be more counterproductive than to engage and pay a publicist, garner national publicity, and not have anywhere for potential buyers to go to hear your music or buy your CD.

A good publicist will map out a campaign generally two or three months in duration (few will work for a shorter period), concentrating on local, regional, or national press. A publicity campaign generally works around the release of a CD and/or a tour. A publicist will develop press materials, advise you on photos, bios, and press releases, and often generate all of the above and have relationships with the music press. (See the "Press Kits" section in Chapter 7 for more on generating these materials yourself.)

The major publicists get major results. As a journalist, I interact daily with a variety of publicists from the major companies in Hollywood to small indie operators. Publicists also specialize; if you're doing speed metal, for example, you won't want a publicist who operates in the cabaret world. $350 to $500 per week for a three-month campaign would be in the ballpark.

Artist's Responsibilities

If you are an artist, you will likely take on many, if not most, of these duties yourself at the onset of your career. This is valuable because you'll have a handle on what each of these endeavors entails, so when you do choose to hire functionaries to take over these chores, you'll know what to expect.

The day of the uneducated artist is long gone. Today's successful artists—whether independent or signed to labels—ask questions. They're not snowed under by smooth-talking con operators or bullied by double-talk. The more you learn about the different aspects of your career, the stronger you will be. And always, if your music is happening and you're making headway, meeting these operatives will come quickly and naturally. Trust your instincts; work only with people with whom you share a common philosophy. Ask yourself, "Is this truly a person I trust to represent me?"

Get a Job

As I mentioned in the Introduction to this book, you will rarely see listings posted for record company jobs because they're few and far between, especially in this age of lay-offs and consolidations. The other reason is that they're generally filled by those within the business whose motion is upward and lateral as executives jump from position to position with the various companies.

In my career, the first position I ever held in the business (that is, not as a performer or songwriter) was selling advertising to recording and demo services and to studios and equipment manufacturers for the Los Angeles Songwriters Showcase *Songwriters Musepaper*. Wages were lowly: a minimal weekly draw plus commission on what I sold and collected on. Initially, I was earning so little in this position that I had to work a part-time job at night to be able to afford to work almost for free during the day. Holding down two jobs was a struggle, but I knew that to build my credibility in the industry I'd have to begin somewhere.

Internships are the time-tested method for the industry to employ free labor. At Cal Poly Pomona, a college where I often teach, most of the students hold internships at labels, music publishing, and publicity companies. It's important to realize that often in order to *get* a job in the business, you must first *have* a job in the business. To work within this paradoxical conundrum, you'll have to start somewhere. Keep in mind that most companies are leery of hiring musicians and songwriters who may have their own agendas.

If you're located outside of a major music capital, you can still meet regional promotional and sales representatives from record labels. The turnover rate in publicity departments tends to be high, so if you can write and talk and are great on the phone, apply in this area. Clips or articles you've written for your local or school paper can be helpful indications of your interest and ability to write about music.

Record labels and music publishing firms are obvious places to apply, but as music becomes a component of more businesses—e.g., coffee companies like Starbucks, retail outlets, fashion designers, and sporting events—a forward-thinking aspirant has more opportunities to advance.

There is little job security in entertainment positions. If this is your priority, you may need to rethink your strategy. Your security will need to come from an ever-increasing list of contacts. If you do land a job in the music business, you'll need to devote yourself fully to the company that hires you, while at the same time being realistic enough to know that jobs are tenuous at best. Belonging to industry organizations, widening your list of social and business contacts, observing patterns and start-up companies—all of these create an atmosphere of information. If you do your job effectively, you will be noticed, not only by your bosses and superiors, but by everyone else with whom you interact. And you'll be on your way up.

CHAPTER 12

It's a Wrap

Personal references will always be the strongest calling card. Being in a position to put people together is a special gift and a valuable attribute for any music business networking pro.

Creative Confluence

I would caution you to always be aware of the balance of relationships between other individuals before you use one of them as a reference. Let me give you an example. When I first began managing artists, a musician of somewhat questionable character told me he was "good friends" with a promoter who handled a variety of outdoor festivals. "Call him and use my name," he urged. When I called the promoter and dropped this musician's name, there was an absolute silence. It took me the entire conversation to recover from this gaffe, and I found myself having to defend myself and my reputation to a stranger because I'd dropped the name of someone for whom he had no respect.

Five Tips for Personal References

1. People prefer to do music business with friends and people they enjoy working with. Become a whole person, not a ladder-climbing opportunist.

2. Musicians are curious creatures; they will often lend their services to people and projects they believe in regardless of immediate financial incentives. Give, take, or barter—"I'll play on your project if you play on mine." All of these factors are advantageous for up-and-coming artists, and friendships and camaraderie among musicians are an enduring force.

3. When you ask someone for a reference, you run the risk of putting them in an uncomfortable position. Although your suggestions may well lead them to that conclusion, it's better if you let them make their own recommendations. Some people like their own ideas best.

4. Notice if others use you as a reference and why. Sometimes it's just a "brush off" and not really a referral. If someone submits music for a project and it's clearly not right, rather than rejecting it, often the confounded listener might interject, "This is perfect for a film/TV placement." This means nothing.

5. Be aware that personal relationships can be volatile and shifting. I was planning to interview a hit songwriter I'd never met, whose co-writer on a top-10 hit happened to be an old acquaintance of mine. The night prior to the interview, I happened to run into my friend, who alerted me to a potential lawsuit brewing between the two and a massive chasm in their friendship. Had I gone in the

next morning and trumpeted my long-term friendship with his co-writer, it would have been an uneasy session.

Back Home

After my first book on networking was published, I returned for a visit to my hometown, Lima, Ohio, where I was interviewed by the entertainment editor of the local paper. "What you've done in your career isn't realistic for most people," he insisted. I disagree: In my world, commitment and resourcefulness, imagination and creativity are shared trademarks of my contemporaries. We work with no safety net, no guarantees, no rules, no predestined career paths to follow down the road to our golden years.

As a teenager, cloistered in my room with musical instruments, magazines, and records, little did I understand how I could forge a career with these obsessions. My father used to remark, "You're living in a dream world," and he was totally correct. I dreamed of living in New York and Hollywood, of a life far beyond the cornfields and oil refineries that surrounded me. Staying in your hometown and creating outlets for your art and music locally is a wonderful thing, too. Not everyone has the same needs. If you love music, incorporating it into the fabric of your life may fulfill you. Teaching music, performing in your local church choir, singing in senior citizen homes—all these are worthwhile outlets for talented people who allow music to fulfill its most elemental endeavor: to make others feel good by sharing the sound.

Making It Happen Where You Are

With the decentralization of the recording industry, it may not be necessary to move to a music capital. Scenes have developed in unlikely places in recent years: Omaha, Nebraska; Akron, Ohio; Austin, Texas; Chapel Hill, North Carolina; Sacramento, California; and Athens, Georgia, being among the most prominent. You can make it happen where you are if there is a sizable audience to support your music—a CD-buying, concert-attending audience—particularly if there is a large college or university nearby. Having local media to promote the music scene, visual artists to identify it, and an audience hungry for culture and enlightenment are all prerequisites to a "scene."

Chris Stamey, who has produced artists including Whiskeytown, Yo Lo Tengo, and Alejandro Escovedo, is at the forefront of the roots-driven sound in Chapel Hill, North Carolina. Stamey lived in New York in the '80s, playing with Big Star's Alex Chilton and forming the dB's with North Carolina refugees Peter Holsapple, Will Rigby, and Gene Holder. But after 13 years in the Big Apple, Stamey returned to North Carolina. "For me, coming back to the South is great," Stamey enthuses. "You gain two to three hours out of every day. It's much easier to get things done, whether it's going to get garbage bags or meeting someone for lunch. You don't have to wear armor as much. I love New York, but it's more fertile for me here." Stamey observes that North Carolina is not necessarily the next musical Mecca. "A lot of things that seem like movements are one person. It might be one club owner making a stand. Here, a couple of musicians bring Wurlitzers and play them in a certain way." But his life, his songs, and his music comprise a compass that has guided Chris Stamey back to North Carolina. "When I was playing with Alex Chilton, I asked him why he didn't live in New York or L.A.," Stamey recalls. "He said, 'Good things come from the provinces.'"

Barsuk Records began as a venture by Josh Rosenfeld and his partner Christopher Possanza to release the album by their band, This Busy Monster. Taking its name from the Russian word for "badger," the label, based in Seattle, is home to Death Cab for Cutie, Jesse Sykes and the Sweet Hereafter, Rilo Kiley, Nada Surf, and many others. *The future soundtrack for america,* a fund-raising compilation with R.E.M., Tom Waits, They Might Be Giants, and others is one of their newest projects.

Rosenfeld explains that his label finds bands through personal references from their signed artists. "We used to accept unsolicited demos. We got too much stuff. It's harder now than it was 10 or 15 years ago. It's so easy now for someone to make music with a home computer. There's so much, it became overwhelming. We started the label because we were in a band and we couldn't find a label who wanted to put out our music. I remember thinking at that time, as I looked at the rosters of labels I admired, that it seemed cliquish: 'Oh, of course they signed you because you know the guys in that band.' I've come to realize exactly how that functions over time. The one huge place where we find music we like is when bands on the roster are on the road, play shows, bring us a CD back, and say, 'This band is really good.' I share a taste in music with bands on the roster, so there is a lot of overlap. It's not a clique; that's how I hear music I like."

What Have You Been Given?

Whatever attributes we have we can choose to use in either positive or negative ways. The music business is made up of individuals who don't fit other models. As I said at the beginning of this book, *Networking Strategies* is not about becoming another person, it is about allowing the light within you to shine and illuminate a career path. As our lives progress, our needs change, and our successes and failures shape our personalities, there are many things that will separate us from music: rejection, changing trends, finite abilities, the lure of the straight job, and partners and spouses who don't understand why we spend our spare time in the basement tinkering with instruments and recording equipment.

With recording artists being signed at progressively younger ages, you can observe that many of these budding stars in Hollywood are managed by family members. "Mamagers" is the newly coined term for stage mothers who navigate their children's careers. Jessica and Ashley Simpson's father, Joe, a minister who traded the pulpit for show business, is now a high-powered entrepreneur. Interestingly, the reverse is also true: Old-school crooner Tony Bennett has become newly hip under the watch of his manager son, Danny, and Tom Jones' offspring, Mark Woodward, has provided the same service for his perennially swinging father.

Maybe your art and love of music will be expressed through your children or, if you don't have children, through those you encourage, nurture, and teach. I hope that the books I write and the courses I teach have helped to enlighten students and aspiring artists—a responsibility that I do not take lightly.

In Conclusion

That plucky poultry of childhood lore, Chicken Little, ran about proclaiming, "The sky is falling!" I hear this echoed by his human counterparts who lament, "The music business is falling!" Let me be clear: The music business is just fine, thank you. Video games, independent films, cable television, satellite radio, digital transmissions, ring tones, remixing, and the rise of independent artists are all adding to this burgeoning bottom line.

There is a tendency to use the terms "record business" and "music business" interchangeably. The record business—sales of music in hard, tangible form like CDs or DVDs—is always in a state of flux. Quite famously, sales of CDs have been impacted by file-sharing of music and the division of the entertainment dollar into ever smaller increments. Back in the day, consumers had far fewer choices on which to spend their entertainment dollars. But the "music business" is much greater than a single commodity. Whenever or wherever individuals make their living connected to music—performing, writing, teaching, consulting, or advising—there is a solid "music business."

As DJs and remixers reinvent the muse, and as samples reconnect the past and future, the soundtrack becomes increasingly cross-generational. New palettes shine from well-burnished hues, and new combinations spin together—punk rockers with country queens, classic rockers with hip-hop artists. The possibilities are infinite. As always, language is being reinvented as the rise of hip-hop fuels the art of the spoken word. As the world becomes smaller, the beat becomes bigger, and music is a potent passport across lines and dimensions.

Everyone feels it, from your skateboarding, Misfits wearing, T-shirted kid down the street to your big-band-loving grandmother. Music is generated every single day to satisfy an ever-increasing consumerism. At the crossroads of art and technology, even dead rock stars are exhumed as classic artists and remixed by today's hottest DJs. Feel the power: Music is the heartbeat. Even Elvis has a new dance hit.

As corporate radio squeezes the playlist ever tighter, a new generation of musicians hunches over computers in suburban bedrooms, roams the hinterlands in packed vans, gives back to the muse in classrooms and choir lofts. We have video games, computers, advertising, cable television, independent artists, digital transmission, satellite transmission, iPods, and pod casting. In my years in the music business, I have never seen as many opportunities as exist today. "Music business" is two words. May the music always come first.

Resources

ORGANIZATIONS

The Academy of Country Music
4100 W. Alameda Ave, Suite 208
Burbank, CA 91505
Tel: (818) 842-8400
Web site: www.acmcountry.com

ASCAP—New York (headquarters)
One Lincoln Plaza
New York, NY 10023
Tel: (212) 621-6000
Fax: (212) 724-9064
Web site: www.ascap.com

ASCAP—Los Angeles
7920 W. Sunset Boulevard, Third Floor
Los Angeles, CA 90046
Tel: (323) 883-1000
Fax: (323) 883-1049

ASCAP—London
8 Cork Street
London W1X1PB
Tel: 011-44-207-439-0909
Fax: 011-44-207-434-0073

ASCAP—Nashville
Two Music Square West
Nashville, TN 37203
Tel: (615) 742-5000
Fax: (615) 742-5020

ASCAP—Miami
420 Lincoln Rd, Suite 385
Miami Beach, FL 33139
Tel: (305) 673-3446
Fax: (305) 673-2446

ASCAP—Chicago
1608 N. Milwaukee, Suite 1007
Chicago, IL 60647
Tel: (773) 394-4286
Fax: (773) 394-5639

ASCAP—Puerto Rico
654 Ave. Muñoz Rivera
IBM Plaza, Ste. 1101 B
Hato Rey, PR 00918
Tel: (787) 281-0782
Fax: (787) 767-2805

ASCAP—Atlanta
PMB 400
541 Tenth Street NW
Atlanta, GA 30318
Tel: (404) 351-1224
Fax: (404) 351-1252

BMI—New York (Broadcast Music, Inc. headquarters)
320 West 57th Street
New York, NY 10019-3790
Tel: (212) 586-2000
Web site: www.bmi.com

BMI—Nashville
10 Music Square East
Nashville, TN 37203-4399
Tel: (615) 401-2000

BMI—Los Angeles
8730 Sunset Blvd.
3rd Floor West
West Hollywood, CA 90069-2211
Tel: (310) 659-9109

BMI—Atlanta
3340 Peachtree Road, NE
Suite 570
Atlanta, 30326
Tel: (404) 261-5151

BMI—London
84 Harley House
Marylebone Rd
London NW1 5HN, ENGLAND
Tel: 011-0044 207486 2036

BMI—Miami
5201 Blue Lagoon Drive
Suite 310
Miami, FL 33126
Tel: (305) 266-3636

BMI—Puerto Rico
255 Poncé de Leon
East Wing, Suite A-262
BankTrust Plaza
Hato Rey, Puerto Rico 00917
Tel: (787) 754-6490

Arizona Songwriters Association
P.O. Box 678
Phoenix, AZ 85001-0678
Tel: (602) 973-1988
Web site: www.punkfolker.com

**Association of Independent Music
    Publishers (AIMP)**
Los Angeles Chapter
P.O. Box 69473
Los Angeles, CA 90069
(818) 771-7301

New York Chapter
c/o Burton, Goldstein & Co., LLC
156 W. 56th St., SUite 1803
New York, NY 10019
(212) 582-7622
Web site: www.aimp.org

Austin Songwriters Group
P.O. Box 2578
Austin, TX 78768
Tel: (512) 442-TUNE
Web site: www.austinsongwriter.org

Baltimore Songwriters Association
P.O. Box 22496
Baltimore, MD 21203
Tel: (410) 813-4039
Web site: www.baltimoresongwriters.com

The Black Tock Coalition
P.O. Box 1054
Cooper Station
New York, NY 10276
Tel: (212) 713-5097
Web site: www.blackrockcoalition.org

The Boston Songwriters Workshop
Tel: (617) 499-6932
Web site: www.bostonsongwriters.org

California Copyright Conference (CCC)
PO Box 57962
Sherman Oaks, CA 91413
Tel: (818) 379-3312
Web site: www.theccc.org

California Lawyers for the Arts
Fort Mason Center C-255
San Francisco, CA 94123
Tel: (415) 775-1143

1641 18th St.
Santa Monica, CA 90404
Tel: (310) 998-5590

926 J St. Suite 811
Sacramento, CA 95814
Tel: (916) 442-6210

1212 Broadway St.
Oakland, CA 94612
Tel: (510) 444-6351
Web site: www.callawyersforthearts.org

Colorado Music Association
8 E. First Ave. #107
Denver, CO 80203
Tel: (720) 570-2280
Web site: www.coloradomusic.org

Connecticut Songwriters Association
P.O. Box 511
Mystic, CT 06355
Tel: (860) 945-1272
Web site: www.ctsongs.com

Dallas Songwriters Association
Sammons Center for the Arts
3630 Harry Hines
Box 20
Dallas, TX 75219
Tel: (214) 750-0916
Web site: www.dallassongwriters.org

Film Music Network
c/o Film Music Media Group
13101 Washington Blvd., Suite 466, Los Angeles,
CA 90066
Tel: (800) 744-3700
Tel: (310) 566-7377
Web site: www.filmmusicworld.com

The Folk Alliance
962 Wayne Ave. Suite 902
Silver Springs, MD 20910-4480
Tel: (301) 588-8185
Web site: www.folk.org

Georgia Music Industry Association, Inc.
P.O. Box 550314
Atlanta, GA 30355
Tel: (404) 633-7772
Web site: www.gmia.org

Gospel Music Association
1205 Division St.
Nashville, TN 37203
Tel: (615) 242-0303
Web site: www. gospelmusic.org

International Bluegrass Music Association
2 Music Circle South
Suite 100
Nashville, TN 37203
Tel: (888) GET-IBMA
Web site: www.ibma.org

International Songwriters Association Ltd.
37b New Cavendish St.
London, WI England
Tel: (0171) 486-5353
Web site: www.songwriter.co.uk

Just Plain Folks Music Organization
1315 N. Butler
Indianapolis, IN 46219
Tel: (317) 513-6557
Web site: www.jpfolks.com

Los Angeles Music Network
P.O. Box 2446
Toluca Lake, CA 91610-2446
Tel: (818) 769-6095
Web site: www.lamn.com

Los Angeles WoMen In Music (LAWIM)
11664 National Blvd., Ste. #280
Los Angeles, CA 90064
Tel: (213) 243-6440
Web site: www.lawim.com

**Nashville Songwriters Association
International**
1701 W. End Ave. 3rd Fl.
Nashville, TN 37203
Tel: (615) 256-3354
Web site: www.nashvillesongwriters.com

Outmusic
P.O. Box 376
Old Chelsea Station
New York, NY 10113-0376
Tel: (212) 330-9197
Web site: www.outmusic.com

Pacific Music Industry Association
501-425 Carrall St.
Vancouver, BC V6B 6E3
Canada
Tel: (604) 873-1914
Web site: www.pmia.org

San Diego Songwriters Guild
3368 Governor Dr., Suite F-326
San Diego, CA 92112
Tel: (619) 615-8874
Web site: www.sdsongwriters.org

SESAC, Inc.
55 Music Square East
Nashville, TN 37203
Tel: (615) 320-0055
Web site: www.sesac.com

152 West 57th St.
57th Floor
New York, NY 10019
Tel: (212) 586-3450

501 Santa Monica Blvd.
Suite 450
Santa Monica, CA 90401-2430
Tel: (310) 393-9671

SESAC International
67 Upper Berkeley Street
London W1H 7QX
England
Tel: 0207-616-9284
Web site: www.sesac.com

Society of Composers & Lyricists
400 S. Beverly Dr. Suite 214
Beverly Hills, CA 90212
Tel: (310) 281-2812
Web site: www.thescl.com

The Songwriters Guild of America
1560 Broadway
Suite 1306
New York, NY 1003
Tel: (212) 768-7902

6430 Sunset Blvd. Suite 705
Hollywood, CA 90028
Tel: (323) 462-1108

1222 16th Ave. S.
Suite 25
Nashville, TN 37203
Tel: (615) 329-1782
Web site: www.songwritersguild.com

West Coast Songwriters
1724 Laurel St., Suite 120
San Carlos, CA 94070
Tel: (650) 654-3966
Tel: (800) FOR-SONG (California and Nashville only)
Web site: www.westcoastsongwriters.org

Women in Music

P.O. Box 441
Radio City Station
New York, NY 10101
Tel: (212) 459-4580
Web site: www.womeninmusic.org

EVENTS

Breckenridge Educational and Music Seminars (BEAMS)

A series of music and songwriting weekends held in Colorado.
Toll free USA: 1-(888) 31-BRECK
(or in Colorado and outside USA: (303) 596-6056)
145 Fairfax St., Denver, CO 80220
Web site: www.beamsonline.com

Durango Songwriters Expo

Currently producing two events: a fall Expo in Telluride, CO, and a Spring Expo in the Santa Barbara wine county
Tel: (970) 259-9747
Web site: www.durangosong.com

Canadian Music Week

P.O. Box 42232
128 St. S
Mississauga, ON L5M 4Z0
Canada
Web site: www.cmv.net

Cutting Edge Music Business Conference

1524 Clairborne Ave.
New Orleans, LA 70116
Tel: (604) 945-1800
Web site: www.jass.com/cuttingedge

Film & TV Music Conference

5055 Wilshire Blvd.
Los Angeles, CA 90036-4396
Tel: (323) 525-2000
Web site: www.billboardevents.com/billboardevents/filmtv

Folk Alliance Annual Conference

962 Wayne Ave.
Suite 902
Silver Spring, MD 20910
Tel: (301) 588-8185
Web site: www.folk.org

Independent Music Conference

304 Main Ave.
PMB 287
Norwalk, CT 06851
Tel: (203) 606-4649
Web site: www.gomc.com

Kerrville Folk Festival

P.O. Box 291466
Kerrville, TX 78029
Tel: (830) 257-3600
Web site: www.kerrvillefolkfestival.com

Music Business Solutions/Career Building Workshops

P.O. Box 230266
Boston, MA 02123-0266
Tel: (888) 655-8335
Web site: www.mbsolutions.com

South By Southwest Music Conference (SXSW)

P.O. Box 4999
Austin, TX 78765
Tel: (512) 467-7979
Web site: www.sxsw.com

West Coast Songwriters Conference

1724 Laurel St.
Suite 120
San Carlos, CA 94070
Tel: (650) 654-3966
Tel: (800) FOR-SONG
Web site: www.westcoastsongwriters.org

Winter Music Conference

3450 NE Terrace
Ft. Lauderdale, FL 33334
Tel: (954) 563-4444
Web site: www.wintermusicconference.com

The Performing Songwriter
Web site: www.performingsongwriter.com

SongLink International
Web site: www.songlink.com

PERIODICALS

American Songwrit er Magazine
Web site: www.americansongwriter.com

Back Stage West
Web site: www.backstagwest.com

Billboard
Web site: www.billboard.com

Canadian Musician
Web site: www.Canadianmusician.com

CMJ New Music Report
Web site: www.cmjmusic.com

Daily Variety
Web site: www.variety.com

Hits Magazine
Web site: www.hitsmagazine.com

Jazztimes
Web site: www.jazztimes.com

Music Connection
Web site: www.musicconnection.com

Music Row
Web site: www.musicrow.com

Index

A

A Chorus Line, 195
absent/present phenomenon, 118
The Academy of Country Music, 229
access, proof of, 56
accessibility, practicing, 108–109
accomplishments, discussing, 64–66
acronyms on e-mail, 123
advertisements, 5
advice, asking for, 96
affirmations, 63
    working the room and, 103
age
    assumptions about, 98
    effects of, 78–81
agents, 216–217
Aguilera, Christina, 41, 182
Aiken, Clay, 178, 180
Air Force 1 and 2, 21
AIR Studios, 16–17
Airplay Monitor, 28
airports, meeting people in, 107–108
Album 88 (Atlanta), 200
alcohol use, 76–77
    working the room and, 104–105
Alcoholics Anonymous, 77
All Through the Night (Robertson), 19–20
All You Need to Know About the Music Business
    (Passman), 215
Ally McBeal, 27
Alpert, Herb, 94
alternative venues, 156–157
Altman, Marshall, 14
A&M Records, 94
"Amazed" (Green), 177
Amazon.com, 32
American Idol, 40–41
American Songwriter Magazine, 234
Americana, 17
The Americana Music Association Conference, 190
Anastacia, 180
Anderson, April, 195
Anderson, Chris, 33–35

Anderson, Keith, 176
Angelou, Maya, 22, 86
Arizona Songwriters Association, 230
Arthur, Joseph, 198
artist's responsibilities, 218
As Good As It Gets, 27
ASCAP, 26, 35, 68, 169–170
    black tie dinners, 90
    compilation CDs from, 167
    General Member Meeting (Los Angeles), 198
    headquarters, list of, 229
    In Los Angeles, 198
    SWAPmeet, 170
    Thru The Walls series, 195
    Web site, 170
    Writers at Night (New York), 194
ASK-A-PRO (SGA)
    in Los Angeles, 197
    in Nashville, 190
Association of Independent Music Publishers (AIMP),
    230
assumptions, avoiding, 97–98
Asylum, 38
Atlanta, 200
Atlantic, 28, 38
attachments to e-mail, 123
attorneys, 215–216
audio engineers, 6–7
Austin Songwriters Group, 230

B

Back Stage West, 234
"Back to You" (Robbins), 179
Baggot Inn (New York), 194
Baker, Anita, 183
Baker, Bob Web site, 152
Ballard, Glen, 22, 94
Baltimore Songwriters Association, 230
bandwagons, 14
banners, names on, 159
Barber, Simon, 146–150
Barsuk Records, 225
Bass, Jeff, 183
BBC Unsigned Web site, 152
BDS, 28
The Beach Boys, 91
The Beatles, 13, 76, 91, 213
    rejection, dealing with, 140

"Beer Run" (Anderson), 176
Beijing, 206
The Bellrays, 23–25
Bennett, Danny, 226
Bennett, Tony, 226
big personality, 45
Billboard, 3–4, 44, 234
    Airplay Monitor, 28
    world chart listings, 206
bios
    example of, 131–133
    in press kits, 129–133
    on Web sites, 149
birth order, 7–8
Bitter End (New York), 154, 194
Black Crowes, 200
BlackBerries, 17, 112
The Black Rock Coalition, 230
Bluebird Cafe (Nashville), 154, 190
Blume, Jason, 191
BMI, 26, 35, 169–170
    Acoustic Roundup (Nashville), 191
    black tie dinners, 90
    compilation CDs from, 167
    headquarters, list of, 229–230
    Lehman Engel Musical Theatre Workshop (New
        York), 195
    In Los Angeles, 198
    Music Connection Showcase (Nashville), 191
    RoundTable (Nashville), 191
    Songwriters Workshop with Jason Blume
        (Nashville), 191
    Web site, 170
    Writer/Publisher Relations Department, 191
Bob Malone (Malone), 186
body language, 87–89
Bond, Sherry, 190
Book of Ruth, 106
Boston, 196
Boston Songwriters Workshop, 230
Boy Howdy, 175
Brabec, Jeff, 36
Brabec, Todd, 36
Braheny, John, 36, 145
breath mints, 104
Breckenridge Educational and Music Seminars
        (BEAMS), 233
Broadway (New York), 193

Brooke, Jonatha, 198
Brooks, Garth, 176
Browne, Jackson, 90
Buckcherry, 170
Buffy The Vampire Slayer, 27
burning bridges, 67–68
Bush, George W., 14
business cards, 102–103
    working the room and, 104

C
cable television, 25
Café Press Web site, 152
Cal Poly Pomona, 44, 219
calendar notices, 134
California Copyright Conference (CCC), 230
California Lawyers for the Arts, 199, 231
Canadian Music Week, 233
Canadian Musician, 234
Capitol Tower, 91–93
career changes, 9–10
Carter, Deana, 198
CD Baby, 148, 150
    Web site, 152
CDs, 17
    compilation CDs, 166–169
    DMI Networks and, 21
    in press kits, 128
    promotional sampler CDs, 167
    signing, 160
    unsolicited CDs, 23
CDWOW, 148, 152
celebrity, 68–69
    strategies for interacting with, 69–71
cell phones, 112
    conversations on, 118–121
    etiquette for, 121–122
Celtic Harmony (Ireland), 179
chance opportunities, 106–108, 139–140
changing careers, 9–10
character traits, 2
Charles, Ray, 18
children's music, 17, 19–20
Chilton, Alex, 224–225
chris and thomas, 33–35
The Chris Isaak Show, 106
Christian rock, 18
Christmas and Holiday Music, 92–93

Church: Songs of Soul and Inspiration, 22
Cinderella Story, 178
Circle of Songs (BMI), 198
clairvoyance, 74–75
clarifying comments, 96
Clark, Tena, 21–22
Clear Channel, 28, 30
cliches in bios, 129
clothing
    information transmitted by, 91–93
    for live performances, 160
    tips, 90–91
    visual cues for, 93–94
clubs. *See* venues
CMJ New Music Report, 234
co-written songs, 36
Cobain, Kurt, 76
Coca-Cola, 21
Cocker, Jarvis, 33–34
coffeehouses, 5
Cohen, Leonard, 94
Cole, Nat King, 91
collaborators, 4
Collective Soul, 200
colleges, education at, 44
Colorado Music Association, 231
Columbia Records, 14
commitment, 12–13
    personality and, 47–48
comparing comments, 96
compilation CDs, 166–169
compliments
    accepting, 159
    in conversations, 98–100
computers, 112
Condé Naste, 21
conferences. *See* music conferences
confidence, posture and, 88
conflicts in studio, 111
Connecticut Songwriters Association, 231
consistency, 77
contacts, 71–72
    multiple contacts, developing, 141
conversations. *See also* telephones
    compliments in, 98–100
    dynamics of, 63
    e-mail conversations, 124
    ending lines for, 100

    instigating, 94–95
    leading questions for, 95–96
    negativity, sharing, 99–100
    sensitive areas for, 97–98
    10-five rule for meeting and greeting, 105
    in working the room, 104
Cook Au Van, 33–34
coolhomepages.com, 151
Cooper, Jay, 216
copyrights, 36
Cornelia Street Café (New York), 194
Counting Crows, 170
country music, 4, 18
    put downs of, 51
    Steele, Jeffrey and, 173–178
cover letters, 127–128
    with press releases, 135
Cover Me (ASCAP), 198
cover songs, 162
The Craft and Business of Songwriting (Braheny), 36,
    145
creative black tie, 90
credibility, 14
    advice on, 64–65
crisis resolution, 81–82
    strategies for, 83–84
crossed arms/legs, 87
Curb Records, 175–176
Curtis, Catie, 198
Cutting Edge Music Business Conference, 233

D

Daily Variety, 234
Dallas Songwriters Association, 231
dance music, 6, 18
dankimpel.com, 146
The Darkest Part of the Night (Malone), 186
Dave Matthews Band, 22
Dawson's Creek: Season 2, 106
Death Cab for Cutie, 225
demographics for music, 78–81
demos
    in Nashville, 193
    placing songs and, 181
    submission services, 39
    suggestions for submitting, 136–138
Denny, Sandy, 33
Denver, Joel, 30–31

desire, 46–47
Details, 94
determination, 46–47
Diamond Rio, 173
digital transmission, 16–17
digital watermarking, 171
Digital Wings, 147, 151
Disc Marketing, 20–22
disco music, 52
Disney, 18
  Cinderella Story, 178
distractions in studio, 111
distribution
  on Internet, 147
  radio promotion and, 30
DIY, 31–32
DIY (Do It Yourself) Convention, 55–56
DJs, 6, 227
DMI Networks, 21–22
DMOZ, 148, 151
Dozier, Lamont, 179
draw, honesty about, 161
drug use, 76–77
Drummond, Bill, 33–34
Durango Songwriters Expo, 35, 201–202, 233
DVDs in press kits, 128
Dylan, Bob, 170, 213

E
e-mail, 113, 122–124
  business cards including, 102
  non-returned e-mails, 142–145
  set-up, copy of, 163
Edison Media Research, 28
education, 43–44
Edwards, Kenneth "Babyface," 72–73
ego inflation, 62–63
8 Mile, 183–184
Einstein, Albert, 59
Eisenhower, Dwight D., 14
"Eleanor Rigby," 107
electronica, 17
Eminem, 183
The Eminem Show, 184
emo, 17
emoticons, 123
emotions
  crisis resolution and, 83

e-mail and, 122–123
and logic, 48–49
telephones, reading on, 114
verbal communication and, 63–64
employment in industry, 219–220
Engel, Lehman, 195
entertainment value, 46
enthusiasm, 45–46
entrepreneurs, 18–19
Epstein, Brian, 213
equity-waver houses, 156
ER, 27
Escovedo, Alejandro, 224
ethnicity, questions about, 97
etiquette
  for cell phones, 121–122
  for studio hang, 110–111
events
  list of, 233–234
  tie-ins, 168
"Evergreen" (Streisand), 185
expanding comments, 96
Expedia.com, 196
extreme strategies, 139–140
eyebrows, trimming, 89

F
facial hair styles, 91
Falcon Ridge festival, 186
family management, 226
Farrish, Bryan, 29–30
Fate, Tony, 24–25
faxing copy of set-up, 163
FCC (Federal Communications Commission), 28
fees, scams and, 164–166
Ferrari, Marc, 26–27
50 Cent, 184
Fight Club, 27
film, 25–26
  independent film, 25
  in Los Angeles, 197–198
Film and TV Music Conference, 233
Film Music Network, 231
Firehouse Recording, 21
first-born children, 7
Folk Alliance Annual Conference, 233
The Folk Alliance, 231
  Conferences, 203

Fopp Unsigned Web site, 152
Fox Music, 26
Frank, David, 181–182
Friends, 27
Fugazi, 28
fusion music, 183
the future soundtrack for america, 225

G
Garageband Web site, 151
gatekeepers, 117
General Mills, 21
generalizations and crisis resolution, 84
"Genie in a Bottle" (Frank), 181–182
Genius Loves Company (Charles), 18
genres, 17–18
Gentry, Montgomery, 173
Georgia Music Industry Association, Inc., 231
Georgia State University, 200
Get Signed Web site, 152
Gigwise Web site, 152
Gillespie, Rowana, 179
Gin Blossoms, 170
Girl Interrupted, 27
Glasswerk Web site, 152
global perspective, need for, 180
goals, defining, 207–208
"Good Year for the Outlaw" (Steele), 173–174
Google Web site, 151
Gospel Music Association, 231
GQ, 94
gratitudes. *See* thank yous
Green, Al, 186
Green, Marv, 177
Greenwich Village (New York), 193
Groban, Josh, 98
grooming tips, 89
Grossman, Albert, 213
growth, impression of, 144
grudges, holding, 142
grunge music, 26

H
haircuts, 89
Hammer, Jan, 183
Hancock, Herbie, 183
Harcourt, Nic, 32, 33, 35
hard copy of set-up, 163

Harper, Ben, 198
Harper Collins, 186
Hendrix, Jimi, 76, 183, 204
herd mentality, 60
hidden opportunities, 106–108, 139–140
Hien, Thomas, 33–35
Hill, Faith, 74–75, 173, 179, 180
hip-hop, 4, 17
    in Atlanta, 200
    Bush, George W. and, 14
    put downs of, 52
Hits Magazine, 44, 234
Holder, Gene, 224
Hollywood, 199
    dressing in, 91
Holsapple, Peter, 224
hometown musicians, 223–225
Horses (Smith), 184
Hostbaby Web site, 151
Hotel Cafe, 34
Howard's Club H (Bowling Green), 162
Hugo, Chad, 55–56
Hung, William, 41
Hynde, Chrissy, 205

I
"I Dreamed of You" (Robbins), 179–180
"I Will Carry You" (Robbins), 178
ice-breakers, 70
    in conversation, 95–96
    on telephones, 118
IMRO (Ireland), 179
in-flight audio entertainment, 21
independent artists, 23–25
independent film, 25
independent labels, 37–38
Independent Music Conference, 233
"The Indie Hour," 30–31
Indigo Girls, 200
insecurity, 62–63
    name-dropping and, 101–102
instrumentals, 27
International Bluegrass Music Association, 231
international markets, 204–205
International Songwriters Association Ltd., 231
Internet. *See also* Web sites
    distribution on, 147
    downloaded tracks from, 145

radio, 31–32
    worldwide market on, 22–23
internships, 39, 219–220
introductions, 67
intros in performances, 161
iPods, 17, 228
It Must Be Love, 106
iTunes, 148, 151

J
Jackson, Don, 19
Jansch, Bert, 33
Japan
    rappers in, 17–18
    Tokyo, music in, 206
jazz music, 92
Jazztimes, 234
Jesse Sykes and the Sweet Hereafter, 225
Jetplane Landing Web site, 151
jewelry, 91
jobs in industry, 219–220
John, Elton, 200
jokes on e-mail, 122–123
Jones, Brian, 76
Jones, George, 176
Jones, Quincy, 68
Jones, Tom, 226
Joplin, Janis, 76
Juicing Room, 146, 151
Just Plain Folks Music Organization, 231

K
Kahn, Chaka, 22
KCRW, 32
    chris and thomas on, 34
Keel, 26
Kekaula, Lisa, 24–25
Kennedy, John F., 13
Kerrville Folk Festival, 186, 233
Kiley, Rilo, 225
The King and I, 11
KLF, 33
knowledge-based skills, 3
Kodak Theater, 185
Korea
    rap in, 18
    Seoul, music in, 206
Kraft, Robert, 26

Kragen, Ken, 81–82, 83
Kramer, Wayne, 25

L
The L.A. Songwriters' Network, 197
LaBelle, Patti, 22, 55
Laemelle movie theaters, 32
lapel pins, 91
Larson, Bree, 182
Las Vegas shows, 154
lawyers, 215–216
Lehman Engel Musical Theatre Workshop (New York), 195
Leone, Bob, 195
Li'l Hal's Guide, 199
Limeys (Los Angeles), 162
listening
    in conversations, 105–106
    skills, 63
Little Richard, 204
Little Shop of Horrors, 195
live performances, 153–171. *See also* venues
    compliments, accepting, 159
    inventing your own show, 157
    peeves about, 160–161
    post-performance tips, 159–160
    soft tickets, 157–159
Liverpool, 205–206
Liverpool Institute for Performing Arts (LIPA), 33, 44, 54, 110–111
local press, releases to, 135–136
logic and emotion, 48–49
logos for shows, 157
London, 205
Lonestar, 177
look, visual cues for, 93–94
Los Angeles, 188, 196–199
    moving to, 199
Los Angeles Music Network, 231
Los Angeles Songwriters Showcase (LASS), 145
Los Angeles WoMen In Music (LAWIM), 167, 232
"Lose Yourself" (Resto), 183
Lott, Roy, 91–92
Loyola Marymount Law School, 199
Ludacris, 200
lullabies, 19–20
Lyric Partners, 19

M

Madonna, 14
magazines
    clothing tips from, 94
    education and reading, 44
    resource list, 234
mailing lists from Web sites, 149–150
Major Bowles Amateur Hour, 40
Malone, Bob, 162, 185–187
    Web site, 186
mamagers, 226
management, 212–213
    dealing with, 81–83
    mamagers, 226
    need for, 213–214
    qualifications of, 214–215
Manchester, 205–206
Mancini, Henry, 39
Manhattan, 193–194
    visiting, 196
Manhattan Association of Cabarets (MAC), 195
Manhattan Transfer, 186
Mann, Billy, 98
marital status, assumptions about, 98
Marketing Your Music Web site, 152
Martin, Joel, 184
Martin, Sir George, 16–17, 111
mash-ups, 17
MasterSource, 26–27
Mathers, Marshall, 183–185
Mayer, John, 77–78, 198, 200
MCA, 26
McCartney, Jesse, 178
McGraw, Tim, 173
McLaughlin, John, 183
Measure of a Man (Aiken), 178
mechanicals, 36
merchandising, radio promotion and, 29
meta tags, 148
Metallica, 90
middle children, 7–8
mingling, 103
moguls, questions for, 210–212
Monterey Pop Festival, 204
Moreira, Rafael, 98
Morissette, Alanis, 22
Morrison, Jim, 76
Motion Picture, 147

Motown, 38
Mouseketeers, 41
MP3, 148, 149
Mrs. Field's Cookies, 21
The Muffs, 25
Mullins, Shawn, 61, 200
multipliers, 32
Murdoch, Alexi, 34
Music, Money and Success (Brabec & Brabec), 36
Music Bridges (USA), 179
Music Business 101 (ASCAP), 170, 198
Music Business Solutions/Career Building Workshops,
    233
music conferences, 201–202
    tips for, 202–204
Music Connection magazine, 27, 198–199, 234
music publishing, 35–36
    jobs with firms, 219–220
Music Row, 189, 193, 234
music stores, 5
Musicbias Web site, 152
musicians, 4–5
    goals, questions on, 208–210
    in international market, 204–205
    Malone, Bob, 185–187
    personal references and, 221–223
    in studios, 110
"My Town" (Steele), 174
mystery, air of, 66
mystical beliefs, 4
myths about success, 57–58

N

Nada Surf, 225
names
    banners for band names, 159
    on cover letters, 127–128
    dropping names, 101–102
    remembering names, 100–101
    for shows, 157
Napster Web site, 151
Narcotics Anonymous, 77
Nashville, 188–193
    moving to, 192
    showcases in, 190–191
Nashville New Music Conference, 190
Nashville Pussy, 25
Nashville Scene, 190

Nashville Songwriters Association International
    (NSAI), 189–190, 232
    membership information, 192
National Academy of Popular Music (NAPM),
    195–196
nationality, questions about, 97
neediness, appearance of, 143
negativity
    eliminating, 52–53
    in personality, 49–51
    sharing negative comments, 99
The Neptunes, 56–57
network television. *See* television
Neville Brothers, 186
New Jersey, 196
New Music Nights (BMI), 170
The New Ride with Josh and Emily, 106
New York, 188, 193–196
    downtown area, 194
    moving to, 196
New York Songwriters' Circle, 194
niche markets, 17
Nile, Willie, 198
No Doubt, 22
non-returned calls, 142–145
North Hollywood, 199
NPR (National Public Radio), 31–32
    Sounds Eclectic, 32–33

O

older audiences, 78
oldest children, 7
ongoing shows, 157
only children, 7
open body language, 87
openness in communication, 108–109
opportunities
    creating, 48
    hidden opportunities, 106–108, 139–140
optimism, 50–51
outdoor shows, 158
OutKast, 200
Outlaw, 173–174
outlaw cultures, 17
Outmusic, 232
outros in performances, 161
over-dressing, 90
overnight success mythology, 73

P

P. Diddy, 200
Pacific Music Industry Association, 232
Paisley, Brad, 174
Parker, Colonel Tom, 213
Parks, Cary, 175
Parks, Larry, 175
Parton, Dolly, 81
Passman, Donald S., 94, 215–216
Paterno, Peter, 216
payola on radio, 27–28
PayPal, 30
Peoplesound Web site, 151
The Performing Songwriter, 234
performing rights organizations, 169–171. *See also*
    ASCAP; BMI; SESAC
    in Los Angeles, 198
    in Nashville, 192
periodicals. *See* magazines
personal references, 221–223
personality, 3
    assumptions, avoiding, 97–98
    big personality, 45
    birth order and, 7–8
    negative traits, 49–51
    success, attributes of, 43–49
pessimists, 49–51
Phish, 28
photos in press kits, 133–134
PHPBB Web site, 151
Pick of the Month (BMI), 198
Pink, 98
Polar Express, 22
politics, assumptions about, 98
Polygram Music Publishing, 179
Pop Idols, 40
pop music, 4, 18
    creative black tie dinners, 90
    put downs of, 51
positive outlook, 45
Possanza, Christopher, 225
posture, 88
power, telephones and, 115–116
practicing networking, 108–109
praise-based music, 18
prejudicial statements, 51–52
Presley, Elvis, 14, 213
Presley, Lisa Marie, 75

press kits, 126–127
  bios in press kits, 129–133
  CDs or DVDs in, 128
  cover letters, 127–128
  electronic press kits, 150
  folders for, 127
  at music conferences, 203
  photos in, 133–134
press releases, 134–136
The Pretenders, 205
PRI programming, 31–32
Princess Cruises, 21
Proctor & Gamble, 21
producers in studios, 110
progression in career, 144
promotional appearances, 160
promotional sampler CDs, 167
proofreading materials, 137–138
proposals
  for shows, 157
  for soft tickets, 158
ProTools, 6, 22
public radio, 31–32
publicists, 217–218
publicity, 217–218
  soft tickets as, 158
publishing. *See* music publishing
Pulp, 33
"Purple Haze" (Hendrix), 183
put downs, 51–52
Putumayo Records, 18–19

Q
Quiet on the Set (ASCAP), 198

R
race, assumptions about, 98
radio, 27–31
  in Atlanta, 200
  compilation CDs and, 168
  Internet radio, 31–32
  KCRW, 32
  promotion on, 28
  public radio, 31–32
  satellite radio, 31–32
  test shows, 30–31
Ragtime, 195
Ramones, 205

rap music
  in Atlanta, 200
  Bush, George W. and, 14
  put downs of, 52
Rascal Flatts, 173
R&B, 4
  creative black tie dinners, 90
Reagan, Ronald, 14
record deals, 49
record labels, 37–38, 138–139
  access, proof of, 56
  jobs with, 219–220
recording studios, 109–111
references, 221–223
Regal Cinemedia, 21
reinvention, 9–10, 58–59
rejection, 140–141
  overcoming rejection, 141–142
reliability, 77
religion
  assumptions about, 98
  praise-based music, 18
R.E.M., 225
remembering names, 100–101
remixes, 6, 227–228
Renbourne, John, 33
repeating names, 101
resources, 229–234
respect
  for celebrities, 70
  networking with, 55
  rejection and, 141
  treating people with, 84–85
Resto, Luis, 183–185
Resto, Mario, 183–184
reversion clauses, 36
Rhapsody Web site, 151
Rigby, Will, 224
Rimes, Leanne, 173
ring-tones, 17
Road Rally, 199
Robbins, Lindy, 178–183
Robertson, Mae, 19–20
rock music, 17
  Christian rock, 18
Rocket From the Crypt, 25
Rodgers and Hammerstein Music, 179
Rogers, Kenny, 81

The Rolling Stones, 5, 76
room, working the, 103–106
The Roots, 170
Rosenfeld, Josh, 225
Ross, Sean, 28–29
Roswell, 106–107
R&R, 30
Russell, Brenda, 179

S
sacrifices, 13
samplers, 6
San Diego Songwriters Guild, 232
San Fernando Valley, 199
Santa Carla Web site, 151
Santa Monica, 198–199
Santa Monica City College KCRW, 32, 34
satellite radio, 31–32
satellite technology, 16–17
Save Ferris, 170
scams
    avoiding, 164–166
    compilation CDs as, 166–169
    event tie-ins, 168
    in Nashville, 193
scarves, 91
Sears Roebuck & Co., 21
self-doubt, 50
self-fulfilling prophecy, 50
self-revealing comments, 96
SESAC, 26, 35, 169–171
    compilation CDs from, 167
    headquarters, list of, 232
    in Los Angeles, 198
    Web site, 171
    Writers on the Storm, 194
set-up, hard copy of, 163
sexual preference, assumptions about, 98
sexy clothing, 93
Shady Records, 184
Shamblin, Allen, 198
"She'd Give Anything" (Boy Howdy), 175
Shepard, Vonda, 198
"Shine" (Robbins), 178
signing CDs, 160
Silverlake, 199
Simpson, Ashley, 226
Simpson, Jessica, 98, 226

Simpson, Joe, 226
Sinatra, Frank, 91
Sixpence None The Richer, 198
sixth sense
    developing, 75
    from press kits, 126
The Sixth Sense, 27
slick sheets, 136
smiling on telephone, 115
Smith, Patti, 183, 184
snopes.com, 123
Sobule, Jill, 198
Society of Composers & Lyricists, 232
soft sell, using, 125
soft tickets, 157–159
"Something to Believe In" (Mullins), 61
Song Biz column, *Music Connection* magazine, 198–
    199
SongLink International, 205–206, 234
Songsalive! Expo, 199
The Songwriter and Musician's Guide to Nashville
    (Bond), 190
songwriters, 3–4
    age and, 80
    in international market, 205
    music publishers and, 35–36
    Resto, Luis, 183–185
    Robbins, Lindy, 178–183
    Steele, Jeffrey, 173–178
Songwriters Club (BMI), 198
Songwriters Guild of America (SGA), 232
    in Los Angeles, 197
    in Nashville, 190
Songwriters Hall of Fame (New York), 195–196
Songwriters Musepaper, 145, 219
The Songwriters Beat (New York), 194
The Songwriters Studio (ASCAP), 71, 198
Songwriters Symposium (NSAI), 189–190
Sony, 176
sound checks, 163–164
soundman, dealing with, 161, 163–164
Sounds Eclectic, 32
    The Vista Street Sessions on, 33
SoundScan, 28
soundtracks, 20–21
South By Southwest Music Conference (SXSW), 233
Spears, Britney, 41
stage patter, 160

Stamey, Chris, 224–225
Star Search, 40
Starbucks, 18
Steele, Jeffrey, 173–178
Stockholm, 206
stolen songs, 56
Streisand, Barbra, 183, 185
strengths, assessing, 3–4
Stroke 9, 170
strong personality, 45
Studio City, 199
studio hang, 109–111
studio/technical personnel, 6–7
Summer, Donna, 52
support positions, 5
swag, 92
SXSW, 25
sync fees, 26
sync licenses, 36
synthesizers, 183

T
t-shirts, 5
tag teams, 66–67
talent, 43
Taxi, 27, 199
teamwork, 212
technical musicians, 6
Ted, 21
teeth cleaning, 89
telephones, 113–114. *See also* cell phones
    basics of calling, 116–117
    ending calls, 116
    gatekeepers, 117
    non-returned calls, 142–145
    power and use of, 115–116
    purpose of conversation, stating, 115–116
    sounds on, 114
    timing for calls, 115
    tracking calls, 117–118
television, 25
    clothing tips from, 94
    in Los Angeles, 197–198
    songs for, 26
Ten Commandments of Design, 151
10-five rule for meeting and greeting, 105
test shows, 30–31
thank yous, 65
    on demos, 137
    to music conference participants, 204
    to performance attendees, 160
    to soundman, 164
"The Way We Were" (Streisand), 185
They Might Be Giants, 225
This Busy Monster, 225
Thornley, Beth, 106–107
Thru The Walls series (ASCAP), 195
tickets, 156
ties, 91
Timberlake, Justin, 41
timing
    and artistry, 13–14
    effective use of time, 54
    personality and, 47–48
    for telephone calls, 115
Tin Pan Alley (New York), 193
Tin Pan South (NSAI), 189
touching base phone calls, 116–117
touring. *See also* venues
    radio promotion and, 29
    success with, 25
Tower Records, 148, 152
Toyota, 21
tracking phone calls, 117–118
Train, 170
training, 43–44
transferable skills, 3
Travelocity.com, 196
trends, 60
The Troubadour, Los Angeles, 20, 154
"20 Years Ago" (Steele), 174–175

U
UCLA Extension classes, 5, 199
ultimatums, 144
UMO Music, 194
under-dressing, 90
UniSong International Song Contest, 179
United Airlines, 21
United Kingdom
    London, music in, 205
    working in, 204–205
Universal City, 199
Universal Music Publishing Group, 28, 178–179
universities, education at, 44
University of Southern California (USC), 14

unsigned artists, 23–25
unsolicited CDs, 23
Urban, Keith, 174
U2, 5

V
Vanguard, 38
The Velvet Rope Web site, 166
Venice, California, 199
Vennum, Bob, 24
venues, 153–171
  alternative venues, 156–157
  as businesses, 162–163
  equity-waver houses, 156
  fitting bands with, 155–156
  inventing your own show, 157
  soft tickets, 157–159
  sound checks, 163–164
  soundman, dealing with, 161, 163–164
  tips for dealing with, 161–162
verbal communication, 62–86. *See also* conversations;
    telephones
  crisis resolution and, 83
viability and rejection, 141–142
Vibe, 94
Vice-Maslin, Michéle, 141, 205
Victoria's Secret, 21
video games, 25
video presentations in press-kits, 128
Village Voice, 196
Villegas, Luis, 131–133
Virgin Records, 75
The Vista Street Sessions, 33, 35
visual mediums, 25–27
visualizing success, 54–55
vocals, 27
volunteering, 6
  at music conferences, 204

W
Wainwright, Rufus, 198
waiting rooms, opportunities in, 107–108
Waits, Tom, 225
Warwick, Dionne, 22
Was, Don, 184
Was (Not Was), 183–184
The Water is Wide, 19
Web designers, 148

Web sites
  bios on, 149
  business cards including, 102
  costs of, 148
  mailing lists from, 149–150
  merchandising on, 150
  requirements for, 146–150
  resources list, 151–152
  sales on, 30
  updating, 148
Weekend Edition, 32
weekends
  performances on, 154
  telephone calls on, 115
West Coast Songwriters Conference, 35, 202, 232, 233
West Hollywood, 199
Whiskeytown, 224
WIFM concept, 2
Wilde, Justin, 92–93
wine spritzers, 105
Winter Music Conference, 234
Witten, Patti, 31–32
WNNX-FM 99.7 (Atlanta), 200
Women in Music, 233
Woodward, Mark, 226
Woolford, Keo, 11
Working Musicians (Malone), 186
working the room, 103–106
WorkPlay Theater, Birmingham, 20
World Cafe, 32
world markets, 204–205
WRAS-FM 88.5 (Atlanta), 200
Wright, Hugh, 175
Writers at Night (New York), 194
Writers on the Storm (SESAC), 194

Y
Yo Lo Tengo, 224
youngest children, 7